The Wheel of Life

THE WHEEL OF LIFE

Buddhist Perspectives on Cause & Effect

The Dalai Lama

Translated and Edited by
Jeffrey Hopkins

Foreword by Richard Gere

Wisdom

Wisdom Publications
199 Elm Street
Somerville, MA 02144
wisdomexperience.org

Library of Congress Cataloging-in-Publication Data
Bstan-'dzin-rgya-mtsho, Dalai Lama XIV, 1935– author.
  [Meaning of life from a Buddhist perspective]
  The wheel of life : Buddhist perspectives on cause and effect / Tenzin Gyatso, The Four-
teenth Dalai Lama ; Translated and edited by Jeffrey Hopkins. — Revised edition.
    pages cm
  Translation of a series of lectures in Tibetan given in London, 1984.
  Includes bibliographical references and index.
  ISBN 1-61429-327-9 (pbk. : alk. paper) -- ISBN 978-1-61429-337-8 (ebook)
  1. Causation (Buddhism) 2. Karma. 3. Religious life—Buddhism. 4. Buddhism—Doc-
trines. I. Hopkins, Jeffrey. II. Title.
  BQ7935.B774M4 2015
  294.3'42—dc23

                              2015028870

ISBN 978-1-61429-327-9   ebook ISBN 978-1-61429-337-8

24 23 22 21
6 5 4 3

Interior by Gopa Design. Set in DGP 11.5/15. Color photographs of the Wheel of
Life thankga by Daniel E. Perdue. Dalai Lama photograph courtesy of Kalleen
Mortensen.

Wisdom Publications' books are printed on acid-free paper and meet the guidelines for
the perma nence and durability of the Production Guidelines for Book Longevity of the
Council on Library Resources.

Printed in the United States.

MIX
Paper from
responsible sources
FSC® C011935

Please visit fscus.org.

Table of Contents

Foreword

THE GERE FOUNDATION is delighted to sponsor Wisdom's publication of *The Wheel of Life* by His Holiness the Dalai Lama.

Winner of the 1989 Nobel Prize for Peace, the Dalai Lama is universally regarded as one of the great spiritual friends of our time. He is the product of an unbroken lineage extending back to the historical Buddha. His forty years as a spiritual teacher and political leader are unique. A brilliant scholar, his words and experience go far beyond the academic. His teachings are rooted in a life tried and tested, a life dedicated to peace, human rights, social change, and the total transformation of the human mind and heart. These can only be achieved through a fearless nonviolence guided by both a transcendent wisdom and an unshakable universal altruism. "My religion is kindness," he has often said.

This book is a wondrous opportunity for us all to make contact with such a man and his teachings. Readers will derive much benefit from contemplating and meditating on them. The Gere Foundation is proud to be associated with His Holiness and his message of universal responsibility and peace, and pleased to support Wisdom Publications in its efforts to promote these ideals. May this book bring happiness and the causes of future happiness to all beings.

Richard Gere
New York

The wheel of cyclic existence in six sectors.

Introduction

WHY ARE WE in this situation? Where are we going? Do our lives have any meaning? How should we make use of our lives? How does Buddhism view the position of beings in the world and the ways humans can make their lives meaningful?

These questions about the meaning of life are addressed in a famous Buddhist painting of a wheel with twenty-one parts that outlines the process of rebirth. The diagram, said to be designed by the Buddha himself, depicts an inner psychological cosmology that has had great influence throughout Asia. It is much like a map of the world or the periodic table of chemical elements, but it is a map of an internal process and its external effects.

In Tibet, this painting is at the doorway of practically every temple. It vividly describes how we become trapped in a counter-productive maelstrom of suffering and how this process can be reversed, showing how Buddhists place themselves in an ever-changing universe of cause and effect. By illuminating the causes behind our situation of limitation and pain, the wheel of cyclic existence reveals how, through practicing antidotes to these causes, we can overcome the painful and limiting situations that are their effects. It shows the altruistic purpose that can make life meaningful. The unsettling description of the steps of entrapment is a call to action, for it shows how the prison of selfishness can be turned into a source of help and happiness for both oneself and others.

THE PICTURE

The Buddha and the Moon

At the top right of the painting as we face it, the Buddha is standing with his left hand in a teaching pose and with the index finger of the right hand pointing to a moon on the other side at the top left. The moon symbolizes liberation. Buddha is pointing out that freedom from pain is possible. (Notice that there is a rabbit drawn on the moon. Whereas many non-Asians see a "man in the moon," Asians see the outline of a rabbit; thus, its appearance on the moon in the painting is merely a depiction of the topography of the moon.) That in the topmost part of the picture Buddha is indicating that liberation is possible sets an optimistic tone for the whole painting. The intent of the painting is not to communicate mere knowledge of a process but to put this knowledge to use in redirecting and uplifting our lives.

The word *buddha* itself makes an important point about the nature of affliction and liberation. The term *buddha* is a past participle of the Sanskrit verbal root *budh,* which means "to awaken" or "to spread," and thus (when put in the context of the doctrines of Buddhism) the verbal root means "to awaken from the sleep of ignorance and spread one's intelligence to everything that can be known"—to overcome ignorance and become omniscient. The general way of making a past participle in Sanskrit is to add *ta,* like the English "ed" in "showed" or "t" in "built." Since to say *Bud-ta* would be non-euphonic, the *t* is voiced to become a *d.* This is how the word *buddha* comes to mean one who *has become* enlightened, that is to say, one who has overcome the sleep of ignorance and has spread his or her intelligence to everything that can be known. The significance of the fact that the word *buddha* is a past participle—"one who has become enlightened"—is that buddhas are necessarily beings who previously were not buddhas. They are persons who were asleep and have awakened; at some point, their intelligence did not encompass everything that could be known. They were, like us, trapped in a state of cyclic existence, going from lifetime to lifetime through the sufferings of birth, aging, sickness, and death.

The Buddha, whose teaching we still have, is considered to be one among many buddhas of our era. Among them, however, he was the only one to make an open display of twelve particular deeds, including his miraculous birth from his mother's side. It is said that he was actually enlightened eons ago and emanated a form called a supreme emanation body, appearing to take birth in a royal family in an Indian kingdom around 563 B.C.[1] He left the princely life and went into retreat in 534, became enlightened in 528, and died in 483 B.C., in his eightieth year, having taught for forty-five years.

Prior to his enlightenment the Buddha was an ordinary being, just like any of us; there is no one who is enlightened from the start. Each of us is or has been in a state of cyclic existence, passing through the processes of birth, aging, sickness, and death over and over again due to our own actions, which are largely motivated by afflictive emotions—emotions with which we afflict ourselves. For instance, when we get angry and our face turns red and contorted, we afflict even our external appearance.

These afflictive emotions, negative influences peripheral to the basic pure nature of the mind, are based on an ignorant misapprehension of the status of phenomena. Not knowing how things actually exist, we superimpose onto phenomena an over-concretized status that they actually do not have. The object doesn't have to be important in the larger scale of life, it can be very small. It can be candy, a slice of pizza, whatever. Before becoming lustful or hateful, ourselves and the object are misapprehended in such a way that a veritable mess of emotions is generated.

The Monster Holding the Wheel

The wheel in the center of the painting is in the grasp of a frightful monster. This signifies that the entire process of cyclic existence is caught within transience. Everything in our type of life is characterized by impermanence. Whatever is built will fall down, whatever and whoever come together will separate.

The Hub of the Wheel: The Three Animals

The wheel itself shows us how to recognize our own condition. The twenty-one parts of the diagram address the fundamental question of how and why we are we born into self-defeating situations. What motivates virtuous and nonvirtuous actions? What are the various types of lives? What is the chain of causation?

The middle of the wheel depicts the basic problem. In the very center is a pig, symbolizing ignorance that drives the entire process. The pig stands for the root ignorance, which isn't just an inability to apprehend the truth but an active misapprehension of the status of oneself and all other objects—one's own mind or body, other people, and so forth. It is the conception or assumption that phenomena exist in a far more concrete way than they actually do.

Based on this misapprehension of the status of persons and things, we are drawn into afflictive desire and hatred, symbolized by a rooster and a snake respectively. In many drawings of the wheel, those two are depicted as coming out of the pig's mouth in order to indicate that lust and hatred depend on ignorance for their existence; without ignorance they are impossible. Both the rooster and the snake grasp the pig's tail in their mouths to indicate that they, in turn, promote even more ignorance—confusion, bewilderment, and cloudiness. Not knowing the real nature of phenomena, we are driven to generate desire for what we like and hatred for what we do not like and for what blocks our desires. These three—ignorance, desire, and hatred— are called the three poisons; they pervert out mental outlook.

FIGURE 1: *The Three Poisons*

Desire
Hatred
Ignorance (the root of the other two)

Half-Circles Around the Hub

The light and dark half-circles just outside the hub indicate virtuous and nonvirtuous actions that are motivated by the triad of ignorance, desire, and hatred. In the dark half-circle are persons engaged in counterproductive actions; they face downward in order to indicate that negative actions lead to lower states. In the light half-circle, persons engaged in positive actions face upward to indicate that virtuous actions lead to higher, or more favorable, states.

Six Sectors Surrounding the Half-Circles

The types of states to which productive and counterproductive actions lead are depicted by six sectors drawn around the half-circles of actions. All six are caught within cyclic existence. Thus, even though the wheel is basically divided into two parts—with three sectors on the top representing the three happy transmigrations and three sectors on the bottom representing the three bad transmigrations—all are equally caught within the round of cyclic existence.

FIGURE 2: *The Six Transmigrations*

(Read from bottom to top)

6 Gods
5 Demigods   } Happy
4 Humans

3 Animals
2 Hungry ghosts   } Bad
1 Hell beings

The sector at the very top comprises gods. These gods lead long and enjoyable lives, but when the force of the virtuous actions that caused them to be born in that state are exhausted, they suffer through being reborn in lower levels. They are especially afflicted by knowledge near the time of their death that their high state is ending and that a low, painful state is about to start due to the fact that they have spent their time in enjoyment without engaging in virtuous activities.

To the right of the gods is the realm of demigods. Their name could also be translated as "non-gods," not because they're not gods, but because they're minor compared to gods.[2] Notice that a tree with plenty of fruit has grown up in their land, and that a demigod with a knife is trying to reach up to cut off a piece of fruit, but the upper part of the tree—the fruited part—is in the gods' land, and he cannot reach it. The gods enjoy the fruit that grows up from the land of demigods, just as industrialized countries take ore and so forth out of third world countries, or as certain multinational corporations live off the backs of poor people working for them. Because their own wealth mainly benefits only others, demigods are particularly afflicted by jealousy and the consequent suffering of attacking and being wounded by the gods.

The sector of humans is on the top left side. Humans undergo the sufferings of hunger, thirst, heat, cold, separation from friends, being plagued by enemies, searching for but not finding that which is desired, and having to undergo what is undesired. Also, there are the general sufferings of birth, aging, sickness, and death. The painting contains figures involved in a range of human activities from butchering animals to living a monastic life. It seems to me that the range indicates that education can take place in a human lifetime. Thus, even if gods' lives are loftier and more fortunate, they don't have the fortune of the improvement that many humans can undergo. Humans often have a mixture of pleasure and pain such that we are not always overwhelmed by pain but suffer enough so that we are motivated to find a way to improve our situation.

On the bottom half of the wheel, we see on the left side the realm of animals, who are particularly afflicted by being used for others' purposes and by their general incapacity for speech. Opposite them is the realm of hungry ghosts, who are particularly troubled by hunger and thirst. Hungry ghosts are constantly looking for food and drink, but they are unable not only to find food, but even to hear the word "food." They have huge stomachs but very tiny throats such that only the smallest amounts can enter; even that becomes unbearable as it scalds its way down the throat.

The sector at the very bottom depicts the hells—the eight hot hells, the eight cold hells, and neighboring hells. Neighboring hells are related to the others as follows: A person dwelling in a hot hell, boiling in molten iron, eventually exhausts the karma that caused him or her to be born there. That person emerges from there and, upon seeing a lovely lake, for instance, rushes into it, only to sink into a mass of rotten corpses. The point is that we find it hard to learn that the very process of attraction and repulsion—which gets us into hellish trouble in the first place—ought to be avoided entirely.

The Indian scholar-adept Kamalashīla, who visited Tibet in the eighth century, says that the sufferings of the six realms of beings are to be viewed not just as occurring in those types of rebirth but also in human lives:[3]

> Humans also experience the sufferings of hell-beings and so forth. Those who are afflicted here by having their limbs cut off, being impaled, hanged, and so forth by thieves and the like, suffer like hell-beings. Those who are poor and deprived and are pained by hunger and thirst suffer like hungry ghosts. Those in servitude and so forth, whose bodies are controlled by others and who are oppressed, suffer from being struck, bound, and so forth, like animals.

My first teacher of Tibetan Buddhism, a Kalmyck Mongolian scholar-adept who had lived through the brutal Communist takeover of the Soviet Union, spent thirty-five years in Tibet, foresaw the Communist takeover there, and emigrated to the United States. He used to say that the Americans were the gods and the Russians were the demigods. In this way, we can view these realms of beings as representing types of beings in cyclic existence but also periods in one's own or others' lives—as short as five minutes, or months, or even a whole lifetime.

TWELVE LINKS OF DEPENDENT-ARISING

In this way, motivated by ignorance—symbolized by the three animals in the center—we engage in virtuous and nonvirtuous actions—symbolized by the two half circles—which leads to rebirth in the six realms of cyclic existence. What is the process, what are the stages of cause and effect?

The twelve parts of the fourth level of the wheel, the outside rim, present the process in detail. These are called twelve links, or twelve branches, because they comprise the causal sequence of lives in cyclic existence. Let us mention them before describing them in detail:

The dependent-arising of cyclic existence begins with (1) ignorance, which motivates (2) an action. At the conclusion of the action a predisposition is established within consciousness, called (3a) the cause-consciousness. This leads—after what can be a long time—to the taking of rebirth, which is called (3b) the effect-consciousness. The beginning of a new lifetime is called (4) name and form. The next stage, the development of the embryo, is called (5) sense spheres. From the formation of the body, (6) contact is developed; from contact, there is (7) feeling; from feeling, (8) attachment; from attachment, (9) grasping; from grasping, there develops at the end of the lifetime a stage called (10) existence, which in fact is the moment just before the new lifetime; the new lifetime begins with (11) birth and then continues with (12) aging and death.

FIGURE 3: *The Twelve-Linked Dependent-Arising*

1 ignorance[4]
2 compositional action[5]
3 consciousness[6]
    a. cause-consciousness
    b. effect-consciousness
4 name and form[7]
5 sense spheres[8]
6 contact[9]
7 feeling[10]
8 attachment[11]
9 grasping[12]
10 existence[13]
11 birth[14]
12 aging and death[15]

Ignorance

The first link is indicated by an old, blind person hobbling with a cane, which symbolizes ignorance. Why? The person is old because the ignorance driving the process of cyclic existence is beginningless; the person is blind because ignorance is obscured with respect to the true nature of persons and other phenomena. The person hobbles with a cane because ignorance, no matter how much suffering it creates, has no valid foundation, it isn't based on the truth and, therefore, can be undermined by wisdom.

There are two types of ignorance: a basic form and a secondary form that is involved only in nonvirtuous, or negative, actions. The first is a consciousness that misconceives the status of persons and other phenomena. It imagines that persons and other phenomena have a concreteness beyond that which they actually have, thereby inducing all afflictive emotions. It is called a consciousness that conceives inherent existence.

Thus, the basic ignorance is not just the absence of knowledge of the real status of phenomena but the active conception of the opposite—that is, the conception of inherent existence whereas in actuality phenomena do not inherently exist. We perceive things as though they were able to cover the parts of which they are constituted, whereas there is nothing that covers all those parts. For example, because a collection of four legs and a top is able to hold up objects, we are deceived into thinking that there is something called a *table* that encompasses those elements. Although phenomena do not exist inherently, or from their own side, or by way of their own character, we conceive them to do so. This is ignorance.

Here in the twelve links of dependent-arising, ignorance refers to the misconception of the person, specifically oneself, as inherently existent, and to the misconception that phenomena that are part of one's continuum, such as mind and body, inherently exist. The person is actually only designated in dependence upon a collection of mind and body; he or she is understood to be merely nominally existent. Still, this view of a nominally existent person does not make the person as if dead or turn the person into the body on which a surgeon operates. When a surgeon cuts open the body and doesn't find any I, any person, he or she might think there is only matter. Obviously, this is not the Buddhist position, even if Buddhists say that persons only nominally exist. Why would we develop compassion for others if they were just dead wood?

The basic form of ignorance is a consciousness that conceives a nominally existent person—a person who actually exists only as designated in dependence upon mind and body—to inherently exist, to occupy a spot in a concrete way, and then conceives of mind and body as inherently existent mine—things owned by the I. The other form of ignorance—the type that is involved only in nonvirtuous, or negative, actions—is a misconception about the effects of actions. In this case, there is also obscuration with respect to even the coarse relationships of actions and their effects—not understanding that if a certain action is performed, a certain result will follow, and developing mis-conceptions such as that only pleasure will arise from theft. This means that if we really knew what it would be like to undergo the future effects of a nonvirtuous action, we wouldn't do it. We wouldn't com-mit murder, steal, engage in sexual misconduct, lie, talk divisively, speak harshly, chatter senselessly, and so forth.

Action

The second link, action, is symbolized by a potter making a pot. If we take our present lifetime as an example, the first link, "ignorance," refers to the ignorance in a former lifetime that motivated the one action serving as the main karma projecting this rebirth. It does not refer to the ignorance that occurs throughout a lifetime, but to the one period—even just a few moments—that motivates a single significant action leading to another lifetime.

For example, if we were in a bad transmigration (that is, if we were not in a human lifetime, which is considered a happy transmigration) the action that mainly generated it could have been an act of murder. In that case, the period of ignorance would be the time in which the murder was planned, carried out, and completed. This period of mis-conception and obscuration would be the ignorance motivating that particular action. The conceptions of oneself as an inherently existent I and of one's own mind and body as inherently existently mine are a cluster, a continuum, of ignorant consciousnesses involved with one action. That action may take only a few minutes; if one is planning a murder, it may take longer. Also, there would be additional ignorance in the form of lack of knowledge of and misapprehension of the effects of murder.

The main action projecting rebirth as a human has to be a virtuous action—restraining oneself from misconduct. Since this action estab-lishes an entire lifetime in a happy transmigration—that is, as a god, demigod, or human—the action must be meritorious because, as

Chandrakīrti says: "A cause of high status / Is none other than proper ethics."[16]

Although there are also causes other than ethics, in order to achieve a lifetime in one of the three happy transmigrations, called "high status,"[17] it is necessary that the projecting cause of that lifetime be an action of ethics. As the late fourteenth- and early fifteenth-century Tibetan scholar-yogi Dzong-ka-ba explains: "This means that...a definite relation with ethics is necessary. If ethics are forsaken, there is no way that these can be accomplished."[18] Nevertheless, ignorance is involved in that one has the misconceptions that:

- oneself, the forsaker of misconduct, inherently exists
- the forsaking inherently exists
- the sentient being in relation to whom that misconduct is enacted inherently exists.

Although the action is virtuous, it is involved with ignorance that superimposes on these factors a sense that they exist from their own side.

To be a complete "path of action" capable of impelling one toward a good or a bad transmigration, an action must have five factors:

- intention
- thought that identifies the object properly
- preparation for the enactment
- successful completion
- nonreversal of intention before the action is completed.

If you planned to kill one person but killed another, that action would be nonvirtuous, and its effects would be negative, but it would not serve as a complete path of action leading to a whole life. What's missing is the actual carrying out of the action with respect to the person you intended to kill. Further, the action must be completed without reversal of the original intention. For example, if the person did not die immediately, and you thought, "This is terrible; I shouldn't have done it," there would not be a complete path of action even if the person died later. Still, the deed would have horrible consequences.

Consciousness

The third link, consciousness, is symbolized by a monkey. In the twelve links of dependent-arising, consciousness is of two types—cause and effect.

Cause-consciousness. When the action has been completed, its potency[19] infuses the consciousness that exists at that time. This brief period of mind, the cause-consciousness, occurs immediately upon the completion of the action. This consciousness is a neutral entity capable of being infused with virtuous or nonvirtuous predispositions; because it is neutral, it can be stained with any type of predisposition. If one mixes together two strong-smelling substances, such as garlic and sandalwood, the two odors will affect each other, producing a garlic-sandalwood mixture. However, if one places something with a strong odor next to something neutral—for example, sesame seed—the neutral substance picks up the odor of the strong one. In this way, the action leaves its own imprint on the consciousness.

The predisposition is a potency, a power, that has been imprinted in a certain fashion (virtuous or nonvirtuous, meritorious or nonmeritorious) and will lead to a future lifetime. In accordance with the strength of this potency, people die at various ages—some people live a long time, and some do not. The potency that mainly led to this lifetime may have been established in any previous lifetime—*any* lifetime, even a million lifetimes or a million eons ago. Then, at the end of the lifetime just previous, the potency for this lifetime was nourished by certain factors (to be discussed later), such as our wishes for the type of life we would like. As a sign that we nourish such potencies, consider the fact that when someone asks, "If there is another lifetime, what would you like to be?" we immediately say, "I'd like to be a..." This shows that we are already nourishing certain kinds of potencies.

Effect-consciousness. The potency nourished in this way is fully activated at the end of the previous lifetime. Between any two lifetimes there is an intermediate state, which can be as short as one moment or as long as forty-nine days. Still, any one life in the intermediate state lasts only seven days; thus, if you remain in the intermediate state for forty-nine days, you take seven different births in the intermediate state.

It is said that during the intermediate state you are seeking a place to take rebirth, wandering in places where beings are copulating, but if you do not have a particular impetus, a potency to take a certain kind of rebirth, there is no way that you can enter a specific female's womb. For example, you may be in an area in which dogs are copulating, but if you do not have an activated potency to be born as a dog, you cannot go into the dog's womb; if the potency that has been activated is of this type, you are forced to enter whether you want to or not. If you are to be reborn as a male, you are strongly attracted to the female, the mother, and feel hatred for the father. However, it is said that someone who is to be born as a male enters the father's mouth or top of the head and emerges from his phallus into the womb.[20] If you are to be born as a female, you are attracted to the father and merge with the mother.

Leaving the intermediate state, you enter the womb of your new mother (if you are taking womb birth). That is the first moment of the new lifetime. It is called the "effect-consciousness"; the term refers to that one moment of consciousness—the beginning of the new life.

In this presentation of the twelve links of dependent-arising (see Figure 4), the first two and a half links—these being ignorance, action, and cause-consciousness—can occur in any lifetime in the past and are called "projecting causes" because they provide the main impetus for an entire lifetime.

FIGURE 4: *How the twelve links are taught in the Rice Seedling Sūtra*[22]

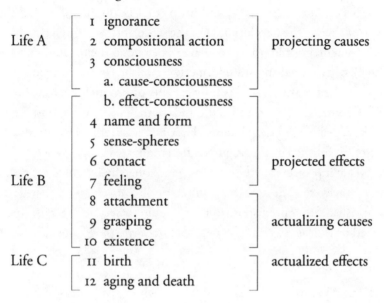

Life A
1 ignorance
2 compositional action
3 consciousness
a. cause-consciousness
— projecting causes

b. effect-consciousness
4 name and form
5 sense-spheres
6 contact
7 feeling
— projected effects

Life B
8 attachment
9 grasping
10 existence
— actualizing causes

Life C
11 birth
12 aging and death
— actualized effects

Life A precedes life B at any time, and life B precedes life C with no interval.

Effect-consciousness and the fourth through tenth links—from name and form through existence—occur in this lifetime; they are called "projected effects"[21] because they constitute the lifetime established by the projecting causes. The creation of a particular life is due to karma, and ignorance underlies the entire process. This being the case, the way to improve lives in cyclic existence is to learn about the relationships between actions and their effects so that we can create more productive situations. The way to gain liberation is to develop wisdom that realizes the actual status of phenomena so that the afflictive emotions that drive cyclic existence cannot get started.

The twelve links, considered in order, produce three lifetimes. In life A, a specific occasion of ignorance motivates an action establishing a predisposition in the consciousness; that consciousness is the cause-consciousness. It produces a new lifetime, life B, consisting of the effect-consciousness, name and form (that is, mind and body), the sense spheres (the development of the sense organs), contact, feeling, attachment, grasping, and existence. Existence is the final moment of life B, when a predisposition formerly established in the consciousness has reached maturity and is fully capable of producing a next birth, life C, which has birth and aging and death. The first two-and-a-half links are called *projecting causes.* They impel a lifetime; the predisposition established by the original action motivated by ignorance impels it. What it projects are the next four-and-a-half links, which are called *projected effects.* The next three links are called *actualizing causes.* They nourish another predisposition to the point where another life, indicated by the last two links called *actualized effects,* will appear.

Name and Form

The next picture is of a person in a boat, which symbolizes "name and form." *Name* refers to the mental consciousness and the mental factors that accompany it, and *form* refers to the body—both of these are located at the point of rebirth, conception. Form, at the first moment of conception, is the egg of the mother and sperm of the father, described in Buddhist texts as the blood of the mother and the semen of the father. The body at that time is extremely small, like a bit of thin jelly. Then it begins to elongate and turns into a substance like yogurt; it continues to elongate, forms the rudiments of a head, and develops bumps that turn into limbs. We are used to our present body, and it seems as though we will always be as we are, but in a short time we will once again have this squishy kind of body. Also, we had such a body not very long ago, but are unable to remember.

Six Sense Spheres

The next picture, an empty house with six windows, symbolizes the six internal sense spheres—the eye, ear, nose, tongue, body, and mental "sense powers," which open the way for the production of the six consciousnesses, giving them power with respect to their respective objects. Here, the term mainly refers to the different moments of the initial completion of the internal sense spheres in the womb; they do not come to full development at the same time. Through the growth of the body in the mother's womb, the senses develop. At a certain point, the capacity to touch develops; at other points the capacity to taste, to smell, to hear, and to see develop.

In general, there are twelve sense spheres—six internal and six external, which are the six sense powers and the six types of objects.

FIGURE 5: *The Twelve Sense Spheres*

Six Sense Powers	Six Objects
1 eye sense power	visible forms (colors and shapes)
2 ear sense power	sounds
3 nose sense power	odors
4 tongue sense power	tastes
5 body sense power	touches
6 mental sense power	other phenomena

Here in the twelve links, reference is made only to the six internal sense spheres and their serial development in the womb, since the six objects are always present. The internal sense spheres are not the gross organs themselves, but subtle matter within them. For instance, the faculty of taste is not just the tongue, but the subtle matter within the tongue that allows you to taste, since there are people with tongues who cannot taste and others with eyes who cannot see. Thus, there is subtle matter in the eye and the other sense organs, which, upon maturation, allows us to see, hear, smell, taste, and touch. Through the development of each of these, there is sensation in the womb. The child moves and kicks, and if the child is experiencing pain, the mother often knows.

Contact

The next link, "contact," is depicted by a man and woman touching or kissing. Roughly speaking, the picture symbolizes the coming together of an object, a sense organ, and a moment of consciousness. Hence contact, in the twelve links, refers to contact with a sense-object and the subsequent discrimination of the object as attractive, unattractive, or neutral. Sense-objects are always present, and thus when a sense organ—the subtle matter that allows you to see, hear, and so forth—develops, an eye consciousness, ear consciousness, nose consciousness, tongue consciousness, or body consciousness will be produced.

There are three factors that cause a consciousness:

1   A *former moment of consciousness* makes an eye consciousness, for instance, into an experiential entity. It is called "the immediately preceding condition."[23]

2   The *eye sense power* allows an eye consciousness to experience and know color and shape. A person can have consciousness but, without a functioning eye sense power, cannot see color and shape. The sense power is called "the dominant condition."[24]

3   The *object* does not produce the experiential entity itself, but affects consciousness, and in that sense it is a cause of consciousness. Without a patch of blue presented to your eye consciousness, it would not see blue. Thus, an eye consciousness perceives a particular object through the object's role as a cause of the eye consciousness; the object is called an "observed-object condition."[25]

Not even the sense organ can act as the *substantial* cause[26] of mind. It affects mind greatly, but the experiential entity depends upon a former experiential entity. When a meditator looks into his or her own mind and feels its continuum, he or she develops a strong realization that mind comes from mind, not from matter.

Mind also does not come from an eternal being; the eternal is permanent and cannot act. Furthermore, mind does not come from nothing, because nothing cannot do anything either. Mind comes from mind. The present mind comes from a former continuum of mind; even when we are in deep sleep or knocked unconscious, there still is a subtle consciousness working.

Though mind comes from mind, there is a long period in the womb when there is no eye consciousness because the eye sense power has not developed. The first moment of eye consciousness of this lifetime cannot come from the last moment of consciousness of the last lifetime since even before the person died the eye consciousness ceased. Moreover, the ear consciousness, nose consciousness, tongue consciousness, and body consciousness disappeared, but the person was still alive. The external breath ceased, but the internal breath had not ceased yet.

A certain yogi who had died during one of my trips to India would have been pronounced dead had he died in the States; still, he remained in the mind of clear light for thirteen days, staying warm at the heart center—the center of consciousness—for those thirteen days. Then, some blood or mucus came out of his nose and ears and the position of his body changed. For ordinary people who die without ravaging illness, the period of clear light is said to be three days. In the United States, however, people are carted off to the funeral parlor before (in the Buddhist view) they have fully died. To be moved during this period is said to be harmful to a yogi, who can remain longer in the clear light, but for ordinary people it is said that it does not make much difference because their minds are out of control.

Following the end of a person's previous lifetime, a mental consciousness travels in the intermediate state; it then takes rebirth in the mother's womb, and, after the visual sense organ develops, acts as the former moment of the first eye consciousness. Thus, the experiential entity of any consciousness comes from a former moment of consciousness.

Where does the first moment of the mental consciousness of this lifetime come from? It comes from the mental consciousness of the intermediate state. Where does that come from? It comes from the mind of death. With that mind of death travel all the potencies that have been accumulated in former lifetimes. This deep mind is a repository for everything we have done. It carries these potencies until they are activated; it is the ground of all the predispositions deposited by our actions—none is lost.

Feeling

The seventh link, feeling, is depicted as an arrow or stick in the eye, a dramatic picture of the centrality of feeling in our daily life. The intensity indicates how pleasure and pain control our activities. While I was staying in a Tibetan and Mongolian monastery in New Jersey in the mid-sixties, a professor of philosophy visited with a small group of students. He asked the abbot, "What do you think students are more interested in, sex or philosophy?" The lama thought about it for a moment and responded, "Sex."

As mentioned above, during the development of the fetus, we gradually develop the impression, through contact, that objects are attractive, unattractive, or neutral. From these discriminations arise feelings of pleasure, pain, or neutrality as the individual internal sense spheres develop. Here in the twelve links of dependent-arising, "feeling" ranges from the first moments of pleasurable, painful, and neutral feeling in the womb to the development of the capacity for orgasm, but it also refers to periods of feeling throughout the lifetime that serve as objects of the next link.

Attachment

Attachment is symbolized by a group of persons partying. This image refers to our desire to hold onto pleasure, to separate ourselves from pain, and our desire for neutral feeling not to diminish. Although we feel attachment even in the womb, the emphasis in the twelve links is on the specific acts of attachment that nourish the karmic potency that will produce the next lifetime. For example, perhaps you frequently thought that you would like to be a certain type of dog, cat, or bird; this attachment activates predispositions for this type of rebirth. (I also wonder whether particularly strong dislike of a person or a group can cause one to be reborn like that person or in that group; one can imagine a situation where, for example, one is reborn in the country of one's enemies from a previous lifetime and even develops hatred for one's previous compatriots due to the attachment involved in excessive discrimination.)

Grasping

The picture depicting the ninth link, grasping, shows a person grabbing at a piece of fruit on a tree. Grasping is an increase of attachment and includes strong clinging to pleasant forms, sounds, odors, tastes, and touches as well as to bad views and systems of behavior associated with those views.

It is possible, at any point in one's life, to have attachment and grasping that serve to potentialize a karma from the past, but near the end of a lifetime these two links are particularly influential in shaping the next lifetime. Therefore, it is said that our attitude near the time of death is very important. If you are lying in bed and everyone around you is moaning and weeping, or if, as they come in to shake your hand, they bend over to kiss you with tears in their eyes, you can develop strong attachment, wishing to hold onto a situation you cannot hold on to. How much better it would be if people were honest and said, "You are going to die. We wanted to come in and say good-bye to you.

No matter how close we have been, lives are lived as in bus stations; we meet people for a while but can't stay with them forever, and now we are going to separate. I wanted to say good-bye. Best wishes to you." If a person could take it, how wonderful! Otherwise, the dying person develops tremendous desire to stay where she or he cannot stay, and this can result in being reborn as a hungry ghost.

As we are dying, we may think, "I'd like to be born as a great general"; "I'd like to be born as an opera singer"; "I'd like to be born as a monastic"; "I'd like to be born as someone who can help other sentient beings." The last two are marvelous!

Existence

"Existence" refers to a fully activated karmic potency, ready to give rise to the next lifetime. It occurs during the last moment of the present lifetime. It is depicted by a couple copulating or by a pregnant woman, symbolizing that the karma nourished by attachment and grasping is fully potentialized and ready to produce the next lifetime.

Existence, the tenth link, is the fully potentialized karmic potency in a person's last moment that will produce yet another lifetime. The cause, the potency, is given the name of the effect, the existence of the new life; the effect is the existence of the new lifetime; and the fully nourished potency—the cause—is given the name "existence."

Birth

New life is called "birth," the eleventh link. The picture shows a woman giving birth, even though the eleventh link refers to the point of conception, not emergence from the womb.

Aging and Death

The last link, aging and death, is symbolized by adults carrying burdens. One type of aging begins from the moment of conception, and the other begins with physical deterioration.

The Import

Those are the twelve links of cause and effect in pictorial form. With the rooster, snake, and pig at the center, the painting graphically indicates that desire, hatred, and ignorance are at the core of the process—the root problem being ignorance. These lead to favorable and unfavorable actions. Those favorable and unfavorable actions lead to birth in the six realms of cyclic existence. The process by which this takes place is the twelve links of dependent-arising, which, according to this system of explanation, takes place in three lifetimes: the first two and a half links in a past lifetime; the second half of the third link plus seven in the present lifetime; and the last two in the immediately following lifetime.

The process becomes more complex as detail is pursued. Just as in this lifetime attachment and grasping (the eighth and ninth links) nourish a karmic potency to produce the next lifetime, so in the lifetime immediately before this one another set of attachment and grasping—not explicitly indicated in the twelve—nourished a potency established by an action (the second link) that was motivated by ignorance (the first link) and deposited on the causal consciousness (the first half of the third link). That potency became actualized in the present lifetime, and during the present lifetime another potency established by an action that was motivated by ignorance is being actualized, later to turn into the next lifetime.

At present we engage in ignorance; on the basis of that ignorance we perform actions; on the basis of those actions we establish potencies on our consciousness—cause-consciousnesses. We begin many complete actions, which will form paths to other good and bad transmigrations. Thus, while one round of twelve links is playing out, others are starting. A potency established in the present lifetime may lead to the next lifetime or to a lifetime four hundred eons from now, whereas the potency that led to this lifetime may have come from an action thirty thousand years ago. In our next lifetime, we will engage in still more ignorance.

The order is definite for a particular lifetime, but different rounds of dependent-arising occur simultaneously. If you break the series into three groups and ask the general question, "Which of these groups came first?" it is true that, with respect to a certain lifetime, ignorance came first, action came second, and cause-consciousness came third. But with respect to these three groups, when you are in the lifetime that explicitly begins with name and form, you are also engaging in ignorance and also experiencing the birth and the aging and death. During the earlier lifetime, while you engaged in the ignorance that motivated the action leading to the present lifetime, you were also experiencing the birth, aging, and death—as well as the name and form, and so forth—of another round.

The motivation for this present lifetime came from one act motivated by ignorance in a former lifetime; this action is called the "projecting," or "impelling," cause. Ignorance, action, and cause-consciousness—specifically, action—drive the lifetime. They established the general outlines of this lifetime—whether we are born as a human or in another transmigration. Then many other actions, called fulfilling actions, filled in the picture—whether we are female or male, attractive or unattractive, born into a poor family or into a rich one, how long we will live, and so forth. One cannot say that everything is predetermined, but we are attracted to a *particular* situation.

When we see that, basically, one action led to this lifetime and that during this lifetime we engage in a great many actions based on ignorance, we realize that we are establishing potencies for a great number of life-times. If we want to end this process, the weak point is attachment, since even if we have billions of potencies to take billions of rebirths, if those potencies remain unnourished and unactivated, we will not take rebirth. It would be like having a room full of rice seeds and not planting them. If we can stop attachment and grasping, we can stop the process of rebirth. No matter how many potencies we had, we would no longer be born in cyclic existence; we would be freed.

To make attachment impossible, we have to overcome the ignorance that is its root. It is through our not knowing the actual status of phenomena and through conceiving their opposite that attachment is possible. Buddhists do not just suppress attachment (although there are many times when this is necessary and there are practices geared for this) but understand something that undermines attachment. Desire and hatred become not suppressed but impossible. There is something we can know that will make attachment inoperative. The basis of desire and hatred is unfounded; it rests on the shaky foundation of ignorance.

Where does ignorance come from? It comes from former ignorance. We cannot assign it a beginning in time, but we can lay out a lifetime, determine its principal causes, and speak of its beginning in ignorance. Nāgārjuna makes these points in his *Precious Garland,* where he presents the twelve links of dependent-arising in three groups—ignorance, action, and the production of suffering—which are called the three thorough afflictions:

> As long as the aggregates are conceived,
> So long thereby does the conception of I exist.
> Further, when the conception of I exists,
> There is action, and from it there also is birth.[27]

As long as the mental and physical aggregates are misconceived as inherently existing, the I also is misconceived to have the same status, as a result of which there is karma; from karma, birth occurs. To restate: The conception that the mental and physical aggregates inherently exist serves as the foundation of the misconception that the I inherently exists; the latter leads to contaminated virtuous and nonvirtuous actions, which themselves induce birth.

FIGURE 6: *The Three Thorough Afflictions*

1 Ignorance
2 Action
3 The production of suffering

Among the twelve links of dependent-arising, ignorance, attachment, and grasping are grouped together as the first of these three, ignorance. An action establishes a predisposition within the consciousness, and that predisposition, when it is brought to the point at which it is ready to produce a life, is called existence. Thus these two links—action and existence—are called by the name of the second of the three thorough afflictions, action. Nāgārjuna calls seven links—from effect-consciousness (in this system cause-consciousness is omitted) through aging and death—the production of suffering.

Nāgārjuna says that three groups cause one another, appearing like the whirling of a firebrand:

> With these three pathways causing each other
> Without a beginning, a middle, or an end,
> This wheel of cyclic existence
> Turns like the wheel of a firebrand.[28]

If you take a stick on fire at one end and turn it quickly at night, someone watching at a distance will see a wheel of fire. Similarly, the movement of these factors is seen as cyclic existence. In sequence, ignorance gives rise to action, and action gives rise to suffering, but they each cause each other. For instance, suffering also causes ignorance; we respond to suffering in an ignorant way; thus, in this sense, suffering is a cause of ignorance, which causes action. Action causes ignorance in that due to actions one tends to accumulate more wrong views, which produce still more ignorance in the future.

When we consider the process of cyclic existence, we see that we are drawn into good and bad situations, drawn into suffering, over and over again, that we are battered and bruised. How much crying do we do in one lifetime? If the tears of one lifetime were accumulated in one place, how large a container would we need? Over many lifetimes we cry an ocean of tears. If we piled up the skeletons used by one person, we would have a mountain as large as Mount Everest. This is the condition of sentient beings.

For a Buddhist, time is not defined by dates and places of birth and death. As a Buddhist, you cannot say that there is any place in the world where you were not born. You cannot say, "These are people I have never known." You cannot say, "I didn't live at that time." Though you may not remember, you feel that you have been present throughout time and space.

The condition of life is not that we have only one life confined by this time, confined by this space. We have met many times; we have been through many different relationships. Value is not put just on temporary experience. Through meditation on dependent-arising, we generate an understanding of our own place in cyclic existence. Once we have understood our own place, we can extend that understanding to others and thereby come to feel deep compassion.

THE DALAI LAMA'S LECTURES

In the spring of 1984 His Holiness the Dalai Lama, recipient of the 1989 Nobel Peace Prize, spoke about dependent-arising in a series of lectures at Camden Hall, London. In five sessions over three days, he presented the basic worldview of Buddhism: how it views the position of beings in the world and how it can make their lives meaningful. An underlying theme of all five lectures and the focus of the last was the fundamental innate mind of clear light. The Dalai Lama describes the obscuration of this basically pure and innermost mind, and its manifestation in the wisdom that realizes the emptiness of inherent existence through implementation of tantric techniques. Indeed, the mind of clear light radiates through his entire presentation of the harrowing process of cyclic existence and also forms the backdrop against which the process is addressed in great detail.

The way in which dependent-arising plays itself out in the nitty-gritty of everyday life is shown in the Dalai Lama's answers to a myriad of questions from the audience. He elaborates on technical issues raised during the lectures and considers many of the difficult problems we encounter in our lives: how to deal with aggression from within and without; how to reconcile personal responsibility with the doctrine of selflessness; how to handle a loss of faith in a guru or lama; how to face a terminal illness; how to help someone who is dying; how to reconcile love for family with love for all beings; and how to integrate practice in daily life. The Dalai Lama addresses these and other issues and concerns with heartening directness.

His intelligence, wit, and kindness suffuse the lectures. His emphasis on peaceful solutions to personal, familial, national, and international problems makes a gentle though powerful argument against choosing allegiance to a particular system as a goal of life. He makes it clear that theoretical systems should be used to serve beings, and not the other way around. He calls on his listeners to use ideology for the sake of betterment.

I served as the interpreter for these lectures and have retranslated them for this book in an attempt to capture the detail and nuance often missed under the pressure of on-the-spot translation. I wish to thank Geshe Yeshi Thabkhe of the Central Institute of Higher Tibetan Studies in Sarnath, India, and Joshua Cutler of the Tibetan Buddhist Learning Center in Washington, New Jersey, for help with the stanzas cited in the first lecture. I also wish to express my gratitude to Steven Weinberger and David Need for reading the entire manuscript and making many helpful suggestions.

Jeffrey Hopkins
University of Virginia

Technical Note

The names of Tibetan authors and orders are given in "essay phonetics" for the sake of easy pronunciation; for a discussion of the system used, see the technical note at the beginning of my *Meditation on Emptiness* (London: Wisdom Publications, 1983), pp. 19–22. Transliteration of Tibetan in parentheses and in the glossary is done in accordance with the system devised by Turrell V. Wylie; see "A Standard System of Tibetan Transcription," *Harvard Journal of Asiatic Studies* 22 (1959): 261–67. For the names of Indian scholars and systems used in the body of the text, *ch*, *sh*, and *ṣh* are used instead of the more usual *c*, *ś*, and *ṣ*, for the sake of easy pronunciation by nonspecialists.

A list of technical terms in English, Sanskrit, and Tibetan is provided in the glossary at the end of the book.

THE WHEEL OF LIFE

The Lectures

The Buddhist Worldview

IRST, LET ME TALK to the Buddhist practitioners in the audience about the proper motivation for listening to lectures on religion. A good motivation is important. The reason why we are discussing these matters is certainly not money, fame, or any other aspect of our livelihood during this life. There are plenty of activities that can bring these. The main reason why we have come here stems from a long-term concern.

It is a fact that everybody wants happiness and does not want suffering; there is no argument about this. But there is disagreement about how to achieve happiness and how to overcome problems. There are many types of happiness and many ways to achieve them, and there are also many types of sufferings and ways to overcome them. As Buddhists, however, we aim not merely for temporary relief and temporary benefit but for long-term results. Buddhists are concerned not only for this life but for life after life, on and on. We count not weeks or months or even years, but lives and eons.

Money has its uses, but it is limited. Among worldly powers and possessions, there are, doubtless, good things, but they are limited. However, from a Buddhist viewpoint, mental development will continue from life to life, because the nature of mind is such that if certain mental qualities are developed on a sound basis, they always remain and, not only that, can increase. In fact, once properly developed, good qualities of mind eventually increase infinitely. Therefore spiritual practice brings both long-term happiness and more inner strength day by day.

So keep your mind on the topics being discussed; listen with a pure motivation—without sleep! My main motivation is a sincere feeling for others, and concern for others' welfare.

BEHAVIOR AND VIEW

Meditation is needed in developing mental qualities. The mind is definitely something that can be transformed, and meditation is a means to transform it. Meditation is the activity of familiarizing your mind with something new. Basically, it means getting used to the object on which you are meditating.

Meditation is of two types—analytical and stabilizing. First, an object is analyzed, after which the mind is set one-pointedly on the same object in stabilizing meditation. Within analytical meditation, there are also two types:

1 something, such as impermanence, is taken as the object of the mind and is meditated upon;

2 a mental attitude is cultivated through meditation, as in cultivating love, in which case the mind becomes of the nature of that mental attitude.

To understand the purpose of meditation, it is helpful to divide spiritual practices into view and behavior. The main factor is behavior, for this is what decides both one's own and others' happiness in the future. In order for behavior to be pure and complete, it is necessary to have a proper view. Behavior must be well-founded in reason, and thus a proper philosophical view is necessary.

What is the main goal of Buddhist practices concerning behavior? It is to tame one's mental continuum—to become nonviolent. In Buddhism, the vehicles, or modes of practice, are generally divided into the Great Vehicle and the Hearer Vehicle. The Great Vehicle is primarily concerned with the altruistic compassion of helping others, and the Hearer Vehicle is primarily concerned with the nonharming of others. Thus, the root of all of the Buddhist teaching is compassion. The excellent doctrine of the Buddha has its root in compassion, and the Buddha who teaches these doctrines is even said to be born from compassion. The chief quality of a buddha is great compassion; this attitude of nurturing and helping others is the reason why it is appropriate to take refuge in a buddha.

The *Saṅgha,* or virtuous community, consists of those who, practicing the doctrine properly, assist others to gain refuge. People in the Saṅgha have four special qualities: if someone harms them, they do not respond with harm; if someone displays anger to them, they do not react with anger; if someone insults them, they do not answer with insult; and if someone accuses them, they do not retaliate. This is the behavior of a monk or nun, the root of which is compassion; thus, the main qualities of the spiritual community also stem from compassion. In this way, the three refuges for a Buddhist—Buddha, doctrine, and spiritual community—all have their root in compassion. All religions are the same in having powerful systems of good advice with respect to the practice of compassion. The basic behavior of nonviolence, motivated by compassion, is needed not only in our daily lives but also nation to nation, throughout the world.

Dependent-arising is the general philosophy of all Buddhist systems even though many different interpretations are found among those systems. In Sanskrit the word for dependent-arising is *pratītyasamutpāda.* The word *pratītya* has three different meanings—meeting, relying, and depending—but all three, in terms of their basic import, mean dependence. *Samutpāda* means arising. Hence, the meaning of *pratītyasamutpāda* is that which arises in dependence upon conditions, in reliance upon conditions, through the force of conditions. On a subtle level, it is explained as the main reason why phenomena are empty of inherent existence.

In order to reflect on the fact that things—the subjects upon which a meditator reflects—are empty of inherent existence because dependently arisen, it is necessary to identify the subjects of this reflection: the phenomena that produce pleasure and pain, help and harm, and so forth. If one does not understand cause and effect well, it is extremely difficult to realize that these phenomena are empty of inherent existence due to being dependently arisen. One must develop an understanding of cause and effect—that certain causes help and harm in certain ways. Hence, the Buddha set forth a presentation of dependent-arising in connection with the cause and effect of actions in the process of life in cyclic existence so that penetrating understanding of the process of cause and effect could be gained.

Thus, there is one level of dependent-arising that is concerned with causality, in this case the twelve branches, or links, of dependent-arising of life in cyclic existence: ignorance, action consciousness, name and form, the six sense spheres, contact, feeling, attachment, grasping, existence, birth, and aging and death. Then there is a second, deeper level of dependent-arising that applies to all objects; this is the establishment of phenomena dependent upon their parts. There is no phenomenon that does not have parts, and thus every phenomenon is imputed dependent upon its parts.

There is a third, even deeper level, which is the fact that phenomena are merely imputed by terms and conceptuality in dependence upon their bases of imputation. When objects are sought among their bases of imputation, nothing can be found to be the imputed object itself, and thus phenomena are merely dependently arisen—merely imputed in dependence upon bases of imputation. While the first level of dependent-arising refers to the arising of compounded phenomena in dependence upon causes and conditions and thus applies only to impermanent, caused phenomena, the other two levels apply to both permanent and impermanent phenomena.

When the Buddha set forth the twelve links of dependent-arising, he spoke from a vast perspective and with great import. He taught the twelve links in detail in the *Rice Seedling Sūtra.*[1] As in other discourses, the Buddha teaches by responding to questions. In this sūtra, the Buddha speaks of dependent-arising in three ways:

1 Due to the existence of this, that arises.

2 Due to the production of this, that is produced.

3 It is thus: due to ignorance there is compositional action; due to compositional action there is consciousness; due to consciousness there is name and form; due to name and form there are the six sense spheres; due to the six sense spheres there is contact; due to contact there is feeling; due to feeling there is attachment; due to attachment there is grasping; due to grasping there is the potentialized level of karma called "existence"; due to existence there is birth; and due to birth there is aging and death.

When the Buddha says, "Due to the existence of this, that arises," he indicates that the phenomena of cyclic existence arise not through the force of supervision by a permanent deity but due to specific conditions. Merely due to the presence of certain causes and conditions, specific effects arise.

When the Buddha says, "Due to the production of this, that is produced," he indicates that an unproduced, permanent phenomenon such as the general nature[2] propounded by the Sāṃkhya system[3] cannot create effects. Rather, the phenomena of cyclic existence arise from conditions that are impermanent by nature.

Then the question arises: If the phenomena of cyclic existence are produced from impermanent conditions, could they be produced from just any impermanent conditions? No. Thus, in the third phase, the Buddha indicates that the phenomena of cyclic existence are not produced from just any impermanent causes and conditions but rather from specific ones that have the potential to give rise to specific phenomena.

Setting forth the dependent-arising of suffering, Buddha shows that suffering has ignorance—obscuration—as its root cause. This impure, faulty seed produces an activity that deposits in the mind a potency that will generate suffering by producing a new life in cyclic existence. It eventually has as its fruit the last link of dependent-arising, the suffering of aging and death.

With regard to the twelve links of dependent-arising, there are basically two modes of explanation, one in terms of thoroughly afflicted phenomena and the other in terms of pure phenomena. In the Buddha's root teaching of the four noble truths,[4] there are two sets of cause and effect: one set for the afflicted class of phenomena and another for the pure class. Just so, here in the twelve links of dependent-arising there are procedures in terms of both afflicted phenomena and pure phenomena. Among the four noble truths, true sufferings—the first truth—are effects in the afflicted class of phenomena, and true sources—the second truth—are their causes. In the pure class of phenomena, true cessations, the third truth, are effects in the pure class, and true paths, the fourth truth, are their causes. Similarly, when it is explained in the twelve links of dependent-arising that action is *produced* and so forth due to the condition of ignorance, the explanation is in terms of the afflicted procedure; when it is explained that action *ceases* and so forth due to the *cessation* of ignorance, it is in terms of the procedure of the pure class. The first is the procedure of the production of suffering, and the second is the procedure of the cessation of suffering.

The twelve links of dependent-arising are thus laid out in terms of a process of affliction and in terms of a process of purification, and each of these is presented in forward and reverse orders. Thus, in the forward process, it is explained that:

due to the condition of ignorance, action arises;

due to the condition of action, consciousness arises;

due to the condition of consciousness, name and form arise;

due to the condition of name and form, the six sense spheres arise;

due to the condition of the six sense spheres, contact arises;

due to the condition of contact, feeling arises;

due to the condition of feeling, attachment arises;

due to the condition of attachment, grasping arises;

due to the condition of grasping, the potentialized level of karma called existence arises;

due to the condition of existence, birth arises;

due to the condition of birth, aging and death arise.

Because this mode describes how suffering is produced, it is an explanation of the sources[5] that produce suffering. In reverse order it is explained that:

the unwanted sufferings of aging and death are produced in dependence upon birth;

birth is produced in dependence upon the potentialized level of action called "existence";

existence is produced in dependence upon grasping;

grasping is produced in dependence upon attachment;

attachment is produced in dependence upon feeling;

feeling is produced in dependence upon contact;

contact is produced in dependence upon the six sense spheres;

the six sense spheres are produced in dependence upon name and form;

name and form are produced in dependence upon consciousness;

consciousness is produced in dependence upon action;

action is produced in dependence upon ignorance.

Here emphasis is on the first of the four noble truths, true sufferings themselves, which are the effects. Then, in terms of the process of purification, it is explained that:

when ignorance ceases, action ceases;

when action ceases, consciousness ceases;

when consciousness ceases, name and form cease;

when name and form cease, the six sense spheres cease;

when the six sense spheres cease, contact ceases;

when contact ceases, feeling ceases;

when feeling ceases, attachment ceases;

when attachment ceases, grasping ceases;

when grasping ceases, the potentialized level of karma called "existence" ceases;

when the potentialized level of karma called "existence" ceases, birth ceases;

when birth ceases, aging and death cease.

This explanation is given in terms of the purified class of phenomena with emphasis on the causes, the true paths, second among the four noble truths. In reverse order, it is explained that:

the cessation of aging and death arises in dependence upon the cessation of birth;

the cessation of birth arises in dependence upon the cessation of the potentialized level of karma called "existence";

the cessation of the potentialized level of karma called "existence" arises in dependence upon the cessation of grasping;

the cessation of grasping arises in dependence upon the cessation of attachment;

the cessation of attachment arises in dependence upon the cessation of feeling;

the cessation of feeling arises in dependence upon the cessation of contact;

the cessation of contact arises in dependence upon the cessation of the six sense spheres;

the cessation of the six sense spheres arises in dependence upon the cessation of name and form;

the cessation of name and form arises in dependence upon the cessation of consciousness;

the cessation of consciousness arises in dependence upon the cessation of action;

the cessation of action arises in dependence upon the cessation of ignorance.

Here, within the process of purification the emphasis is on the effects—true cessations, the third of the four noble truths.

These processes are depicted in a painting called the wheel of cyclic existence with five sectors[6] (see plates 1–7). Within cyclic existence, gods and demigods are combined in one sector; then there is a sector of humans; these three are known as the happy transmigrations, depicted in the top half of the wheel. The three sectors in the bottom half are bad or low transmigrations—those of animals, hungry ghosts, and hell-beings. All of these sectors represent the levels of suffering in terms of types of birth.

Due to what conditions do these forms of suffering arise? The circle just inside the five sectors of beings indicates that these levels of suffering are produced by karma—by actions. It is in two halves. The half on the right, which has a white base with people looking and moving upward, symbolizes virtuous actions, these being of two types, meritorious and unfluctuating; such actions are the means of attaining lives as humans, demigods, and gods. The left half, which has a dark base with people facing downward, symbolizes nonvirtuous actions, which impel beings toward lifetimes in the lower realms.

From what do these karmas that are the sources of suffering arise? They stem from a further source of suffering—the afflictive emotions of desire, hatred, and ignorance—indicated by the innermost circle where a pig, a snake, and a rooster are depicted. The pig symbolizes ignorance; the snake, hatred; and the rooster, desire. In some versions of the painting, the pig grasps the tails of the rooster and the snake in its mouth, thereby indicating that desire and hatred have ignorance as their root. Also, the rooster and the snake grasp the tail of the pig in their mouths to indicate that each of them acts to assist and further the other.

Symbolically these three circles, moving from the center outward, show that the three afflictive emotions of desire, hatred, and ignorance give rise to virtuous and nonvirtuous actions, which, in turn, give rise to the various levels of suffering in cyclic existence. The outer rim symbolizing the twelve links of dependent-arising indicates *how* the sources of suffering—actions and afflictive emotions— produce lives within cyclic existence. The fierce being holding the wheel symbolizes impermanence, which is why the being is a wrathful monster, though there is no need for it to be drawn with ornaments and so forth as it is here. Once I had such a painting drawn with a skeleton rather than a monster, in order to symbolize impermanence more clearly.

The moon on the far right side indicates liberation. The Buddha on the left is pointing to the moon, indicating that the liberation that causes one to cross the ocean of suffering of cyclic existence should be actualized.

With regard to the history of this painting, at the time of Shākyamuni Buddha, an outlying king, Udāyana, made a present of a jeweled robe to the king of Magadha, Bimbisāra, who did not have anything of equivalent worth to give in return. Bimbisāra was worried about this and asked the Buddha what he should give. The Buddha indicated that he should have a wheel of cyclic existence with five sectors drawn accompanied by the following:

> Undertaking this and leaving that,
> Enter into the teaching of the Buddha.
> Like an elephant in a thatch house,
> Destroy the forces of the Lord of Death.
> Those who with thorough conscientiousness
> Practice this disciplinary doctrine
> Will forsake the wheel of birth,
> Bringing suffering to an end.

The Buddha told Bimbisāra to send this to King Udāyana. It is said that when the king received the picture and studied it, he attained realization.[7]

The twelve links of dependent-arising are symbolized by the twelve pictures around the outside. The first, at the top—an old person, blind and hobbling with a cane—symbolizes ignorance, the first link. In this context, ignorance is obscuration with respect to the actual mode of being of phenomena. Since within the Buddhist philosophical schools there are four main systems of tenets and, within those schools, there are many different divisions, there are many interpretations of what ignorance is. Not only do we not have time to discuss all of these, I do not even remember all of them!

One type of ignorance is the mere non-knowing of how things actually exist, a factor of mere obscuration. However, here in the twelve links of dependent-arising, ignorance is explained as a wrong consciousness that conceives the opposite of how things actually do exist.

Ignorance is the chief of the afflictive emotions that we are seeking to abandon. Each afflictive emotion is of two types: innate and intellectually acquired. Intellectually acquired afflictive emotions are based on inadequate systems of tenets, such that the mind imputes or fosters new afflictive emotions through conceptuality. These are not afflictive emotions that all sentient beings have and cannot be the ones that are at the root of the ruination of beings. As Nāgārjuna says in his *Seventy Stanzas on Emptiness*:

> That consciousness that conceives things
> Which are produced in dependence upon
> Causes and conditions
> To ultimately exist
> Was said by the Teacher to be ignorance.
> From it the twelve links arise.[8]

This is a consciousness that *innately* misapprehends, or misconceives, phenomena as existing under their own power, as not dependent.

Because this consciousness has different types of objects, ignorance is divided into two types: one that conceives inherent existence upon observing persons and another type that conceives inherent existence upon observing other phenomena. These are called consciousnesses that conceive, respectively, a self of persons and a self of phenomena.

The conception of a self of persons is of two types: the first is to take cognizance of one's own person, one's own I, and consider oneself

The Buddhist Worldview 45

to be inherently existent. The second, coarser type of conception of a self of persons is where one misapprehends other persons as being substantially existent in the sense of being self-sufficient. The former is called "the false view of the transitory collection."[9] In the stanza cited above, Nāgārjuna indicates that the innate false view of the transitory collection, which is the root of cyclic existence, is the conception of one's own self as inherently existent and that it arises in dependence upon the conception of those mental and physical aggregates that are the bases of designation of oneself—one's mind, body, and so forth— as inherently existent. In this way, the conception of a self of phenomena acts as a basis for the innate false view of the transitory collection that is a conception of the person as inherently existent, even though both types are ignorant consciousnesses that conceive inherent existence.

When we reflect on our own desire and hatred, we see that they are generated within a conception of oneself as very solid, due to which there arises a strong distinction between oneself and others, and consequently, attachment to one's self and hatred for others. Attitudes of desire and hatred are all based on an exaggerated sense of I, are they not?

There is indeed a conventionally posited, valid I—a self that is the doer of actions, that is the accumulator of karma, and that is the person undergoing the pleasure and pain that are the fruit of those actions. However, when we examine the mode of apprehension of the mind when the I becomes a troublemaker, we find that we are conceiving a self-instituting I that is an exaggeration beyond what actually exists. When this I appears to the mind, it does not appear to be designated in dependence upon the aggregates of mind and body; rather, it seems almost as if it is its own separate entity. If it were to exist in such a solid, independent way, then when one investigates it with the Middle Way reasoning,[10] it should become clearer and clearer, but in fact the opposite happens, such that it becomes less and less clear until it cannot be found. If it were so concrete and independent, it would be findable under analysis. The fact that it cannot be found indicates that, except for its mere designation in dependence upon the coming together of certain circumstances, it does not exist. Still, it appears to our minds to be something that can be indicated concretely, but when we assent to this false appearance, we get into trouble.

The conflict between the concrete appearance of the I and the fact that, when analyzed, it cannot be found indicates a discrepancy between its appearance and how it actually exists. Physicists make a similar distinction between what appears and what actually exists.

In our own experience, we can identify types or levels of desire. When we see a certain article in a store and have a desire for it, that constitutes an initial type of desire, but after we buy it and feel, "This is mine," this is a different level. They are similar in both being attitudes of desire, but they differ in strength.

It is important to distinguish three levels of appearance and apprehension. In the first level, when mere appearance and mere recognition of the object occur, the object merely appears, without generating desire. Then, when we feel, "Oh, this is really good," and desire has been generated, this is another level of appearance and apprehension of the object. Upon deciding to buy the article and making it our own, cherishing it as our own, there is a third level of appearance and apprehension.

On the first level, which consists of the mere appearance of the object, the object does seem to exist inherently; however, the mind is not strongly involved with the object. On the second level, desire for the object is induced by ignorance that apprehends it as existing inherently. There is a subtle level of desire that can exist at the same time as this consciousness that conceives the object to exist inherently, but when desire becomes stronger, the conception of inherent existence acts as its cause, inducing still more desire, but does not exist at exactly the same time as desire. It is crucial to realize from your own experience that:

◆ on the first level there is the appearance of the object as inherently existent;

◆ on the second level there is a consciousness that assents to this appearance, apprehending the object as inherently existent and thus giving rise to desire;

◆ on the third level, when we have bought such an inherently pleasing object and made it our own, the object becomes involved with a strong conception of ownership in which we consider it to be extremely valuable.

At the end of this process two very powerful streams of adherence—attachment for the inherently pleasant object and attachment for oneself—have come together, making the desire even greater than before. Reflect on whether or not this is so.

The same is true of hatred. There is an initial experience involving a conventionally valid perception of the qualities of an object—for instance, seeing something bad and identifying it as bad. Then one produces hatred upon thinking, "Oh, this is really bad," this is a second level. When the hatred is related to oneself, it is stronger, and when it is seen as potentially bringing harm to oneself, even stronger hatred develops.

Thus, the ignorance that is the conception of inherent existence acts to assist both desire and hatred. In this way, the cause of all this trouble is the pig! And in the Tibetan calendar the year of my birth is the Year of the Pig!

This is the way obscuration—ignorance—serves as the root of the other afflictive emotions. This ignorant consciousness is obscured with respect to the mode of being of phenomena, and hence it is symbolized in the painting by a blind person. Also, since ignorance is weak in the sense that it is not founded upon valid cognition, the person hobbles using a cane. More properly, ignorance should be depicted at the bottom of the painting, but it is often put at the top.

In dependence upon such ignorance, the second of the twelve links of dependent-arising, action, occurs. It is called *compositional* action because actions serve to compose or bring about pleasurable and painful effects. It is symbolized by a potter. A potter takes clay and forms it into a new article, and similarly an action begins a sequence that leads to new consequences. Also, once the potter spins the wheel,[11] it will keep turning as long as is needed without further striving and exertion; similarly, when an action has been done by a sentient being, it establishes a predisposition in the mind—or as is said in the Consequence School, it produces a state of destructedness of that action—and this predisposition or state of destructedness has the potential to continue unhindered until it produces its effect.

Considering the effects of actions in terms of consequent rebirths in the desire, form, and formless realms, there are virtuous actions and nonvirtuous actions, and within virtuous actions there are meritorious actions and nonfluctuating actions. In terms of the way in which they are performed, there are actions of body, speech, and mind. In terms of their own entities, there are actions of intention[12] and intended actions.[13] There are also definite and indefinite actions indicating whether or not the effect is definitely to be experienced. With regard to the former, the effects can be experienced in this lifetime, the next, or a later one.

Also, taking a human lifetime as an example, there are actions that impel or project one's bodily life in a general way and there are other types of actions that fill in the picture, so to speak, which are called completing actions. These fill in the specific details—for instance, causing one's body to be beautiful, ugly, and so forth. Consider a human who undergoes many illnesses; as in the case of all other humans, the projecting or impelling karma was a virtuous action, as can be determined by the mere fact that the person was born as a human. The completing actions that fill in the picture by creating a propensity for disease are nonvirtuous actions. The opposite occurs when the impelling karma is nonvirtuous and the completing actions filling in the picture are virtuous, as in the case of an animal with a good, healthy body. There are also cases in which both the impelling and completing actions are virtuous, as well as the opposite case in which both are nonvirtuous.

Another division of actions distinguishes those done deliberately, those deliberated but not done, those done but not deliberately, and those neither deliberated nor done.[14] Also, there are actions in which (1) the thought is wholesome but the execution of the action is unwholesome, (2) the thought is unwholesome but the execution of it is wholesome, (3) both the thought and the execution are unwholesome, or (4) both the thought and the execution are wholesome. Again, there are actions whose effects are experienced in common by a number of beings and actions whose effects are experienced only by one individual.

How are karmas accumulated? For example, one particular motivation may lead to certain physical and verbal actions. Good motivation leads to nice words and gentle physical actions, whereby good karma is accumulated. An immediate result is felt in the creation of a peaceful, friendly atmosphere. However, anger motivates rude words and harsh physical and verbal actions, immediately creating an unpleasant atmosphere. In both cases an action is produced with ignorance of the final nature of phenomena as the background; this is the first stage of a karma. When the action ceases, it imprints a potency, a predisposition, into the consciousness, and the continuum of the consciousness carries this potency to the time of the fruition of that karma. In this way, an action creates both an immediate result and a potential that eventually brings about either a pleasant or a painful experience in the future.

This is how the first link, ignorance, motivates the second link, action, which establishes a potency for future experience in the third link, consciousness. Consciousness is symbolized by a picture of a monkey. Within Buddhism there are several interpretations of the number of consciousnesses; one system posits only one; others posit six; another posits eight; and another, nine. Although most Buddhist systems posit six types of consciousness, the picture is often one of a monkey going from window to window in a house; it probably has its origins in the positing of only one consciousness. When this single consciousness perceives by way of the eye, it seems to be an eye-consciousness, and when it perceives by way of the ear, nose, tongue, and body, it seems respectively to be an ear-consciousness, nose-consciousness, tongue-consciousness, and body-consciousness; but it, like the single monkey at many windows, is only one. In any case, a monkey is a clever and active animal and thus can symbolize these qualities of consciousness.

A problem is that between an action and its fruition there can be a considerable period of time, yet all Buddhist systems assert that karmas are not lost or wasted; between the cause and the effect there must be something that connects the two. Many different assertions are presented within the Buddhist systems regarding what connects an action with its long-range effect. The best solution is offered in the Consequence School, as follows: All systems posit that there is a person at the time an action is performed and at the time its effect is experienced. Thus there must be a continuum of a dependently imputed I—which provides the basis for the infusion of the predisposition[15] created by an action. As long as a system is unable to present such a basis for infusion of predispositions, it has to find an independently identifiable basis for infusion of those potencies; this is why the Mind Only School posits a mind-basis-of-all[16] as the basis for infusion of predispositions. However, the highest system, the Consequence School, has no such difficulty since it holds that the continual basis of infusion of predispositions is the mere I, the mere person, and that the temporary basis for infusion of predispositions is consciousness.

In this way, immediately after an action, there is a state of destructedness or cessation of that action, which, it could be said, turns into the entity of a predisposition infused in consciousness. The consciousness extending from this moment until just before the moment of conception in the new lifetime is called the consciousness of the causal time or cause-consciousness. The consciousness of the very next moment, in which connection to the next lifetime is made, is called the effect-consciousness. In terms of its duration, the effect-consciousness lasts from that moment to just before the time of the fourth link, name and form, and thus is extremely brief.

Concerning name and form, "name" refers to the four mental aggregates of feeling, discrimination, compositional factors, and consciousness. "Form" is the aggregate of physical phenomena. In our painting, it is depicted by people riding in a boat; in other pictures, it is symbolized by poles that lean against each other. The latter stems from a scripture teaching the Mind Only presentation of (1) a mental consciousness, (2) a mind-basis-of-all, and (3) a form, which are like the legs of a tripod supporting each other. In our depiction, the boat symbolizes form, and the people in the boat symbolize the mental aggregates. The period of name and form continues during the development of the embryo until it begins to develop the five organs.

QUESTIONS

Question: Could you clarify the two types of analytical meditation.

Answer: Both analytical meditation and stabilizing meditation are of two types. In the first type of analytic meditation, you are meditating *on* an object, as is the case when meditating on impermanence; in the second, you are causing your own consciousness to be generated into a state of mind, such as when meditatively cultivating love. When you meditate on impermanence or emptiness, you are taking these as the object of your mind, but when you "meditate" faith or "meditate" compassion, you are not meditating on faith or on compassion through reflecting on their qualities; rather, you are generating your own consciousness into a faithful or compassionate consciousness.

Question: How many types of analytical investigation are there?

Answer: Within the Buddhist systems there are four ways of investigating phenomena. The first is to look into the functions that an object performs, for example, that fire burns or water moistens; the next is to investigate by way of reasoning based on valid proof; the third is to look into dependence, as in causation; and the last is the reasoning of looking into just the nature of the object, that something is naturally so. I think there are many phenomena that must be understood in the context of the fourth type of rational inquiry—of its just being the nature of something to be so. It strikes me that this type of reasoning may be used in connection with the topic of karmic causation; for instance, if one harms someone else, then because the nature of that action is to bring harm to a sentient being, the result naturally is that harm returns to oneself. Similarly, because helping another sentient being has a nature of bringing benefit, the effect that returns to oneself is also beneficial.

Also, if one asks why consciousness has the character of experiencing objects or why physical objects are material, one can look into their respective substantial causes and cooperative conditions, but when one moves the question further and further back, it is probably just that it is the nature of consciousness to be an entity of experience. If one posited a beginning to consciousness, that position would be exposed to much damage by reasoning; for instance, it would be absurd to claim that a luminous and cognitive entity could be produced by something that is not a luminous and cognitive entity. Since there are many such contradictions in that position, it is better to take the position that there is no beginning to consciousness.

With regard to particles of matter, consciousness may be able to serve as a cooperative condition in the process of producing matter, but its substantial cause must be something material since matter must be produced from something of a similar type. For instance, consider our own galaxy, or world-system of one billion worlds. In the traditional Buddhist presentation there are eons of vacuity, then eons of formation, eons of abiding, and eons of destruction; this series of four phases goes on and on and on, over and over again without end. I wonder whether the substances that produce the particles that are the building blocks during the period of formation are present during the period of the eons of vacuity. Perhaps the particles of space mentioned in the Kālachakra system refer to this. Even if five or six billion years have passed since the Big Bang, there needs to be an explanation of what prior causal conditions gave rise to it.

From another point of view, there are yogis who cultivate meditative states called the earth-totality, water-totality, and so forth, in which all that appears is just earth or just water, and so forth. Also, the phenomena that are produced through the power of yoga indeed have no limit. For instance, even though we have to posit solidity, things cannot be posited as solid in all respects and in terms of all situations; rather, they are posited as solid only in relation to a particular situation.

Question: Please give your definition of "I," the self.

Answer: Those who do not have any belief in former and future lifetimes may not pay much attention to what the entity or nature of the self is, but among those who do have such a belief there are many different assertions. Many non-Buddhist systems posit a permanent self that continues from lifetime to lifetime. They do this because they see that something goes from one life to another and that clearly the body does not; they cannot posit something impermanent that continues from life to life, so they posit a permanent, unitary, and independent self that travels from one life to the next.

Within the Buddhist systems, an I is posited, but not in the same way as above. Feeling that the I, or self, must be something that can be posited upon analysis, the lower Buddhist systems hold that something *from within* the impermanent collection of mind and body must be posited as the I, or self. Certain of these Buddhist schools posit the mental consciousness; some posit the mind-basis-of-all; some, the continuum of the aggregates; and so forth. However, the supreme of all Buddhist tenet systems, the Consequence School, holds that just as a chariot is imputed in dependence upon its parts and cannot be found among the parts themselves, so a person is merely imputed in dependence upon the mental and physical aggregates but cannot be found, under analysis, among any of those aggregates. Thus, not only is the I dependently imputed, but all phenomena are dependently imputed; even emptiness is dependently imputed, as is buddhahood—all appearing and occurring phenomena are just dependently designated.

Question: Your Holiness, could you talk about the connection between the five aggregates and the five elements.

Answer: First it is necessary to identify the five aggregates; these are forms, feelings, discriminations, compositional factors, and consciousnesses. Within the form aggregate the coarser level is, for instance, our body of flesh, blood, and so forth, and the more subtle levels involve the topic of various winds, or inner energies, described in highest yoga tantra. In tantra, there are many explanations of connections between the movement of basic physical constituents and inner energies, or winds, in channels whereby different levels of consciousness, conceptual and nonconceptual, are produced.[17]

The remaining four aggregates are called "the bases of the name."[18] These are feeling, discrimination, compositional factors, and consciousness. The aggregate of feeling and the aggregate of discrimination are the mental factors of feeling and discrimination, which are distinguished from all other mental factors.[19] In the *Treasury of Manifest Knowledge*,[20] Vasubandhu explains that this distinction occurs because discrimination is the source of all dispute, and because one is drawn into afflictive actions and hence into cyclic existence by attachment to pleasurable feeling and attachment to wanting to be separate from painful feeling. Within the fourth aggregate, compositional factors, there are two main types: compositional factors associated with consciousness and those not associated with consciousness. In general, when we speak about beings with a physical body, they have all five aggregates, but in the formless realm there are only the four mental aggregates. From the viewpoint of highest yoga tantra, however, this is only in terms of coarse form.

There are four basic elements of earth, water, fire, and wind. The first, though termed "earth," refers mainly to solidity and obstructiveness. "Water" refers to fluidity and moistening. "Fire" means heat and burning. In coarse terms, "wind" refers to the air that we breathe in and out, but on a subtle level it refers mainly to types of energies that promote development and change. For instance, in the Kālachakra system it is said that even a dead body still has winds functioning in it, because it continues to undergo change. An additional element is space, which, in reference to the body, means empty cavities and passageways. The Kālachakra system also speaks of particles of space, which are extremely subtle; scientists similarly speak of minute particles in space that serve as a basis for other phenomena.

Those are the five aggregates and the five elements. If you have other questions about these topics, please ask.

Question: Since all appearances and all life are just illusion, is it not inconsistent to say that there are levels of appearance, such as those you mentioned this morning?

Answer: It is not that life *is* an illusion; rather, it is *like* an illusion. Therefore, we can speak of many different types of discrepancy between the way things appear and the way they actually exist. For instance, something that is actually impermanent can appear to be permanent; sometimes things that are actually sources of pain appear to be sources of pleasure. These are types of conflict between the way things actually are and the way they appear. As regards final reality, objects appear to exist inherently but actually lack inherent existence; this is another level of discrepancy between appearance and fact.

Question: How does belief or disbelief relate to ignorance?

Answer: Mostly we have the belief that objects inherently exist; they appear to exist from their own side, and we believe that they exist this way. This type of belief is induced by ignorance.

Question: When is desire cause and when is desire effect?

Answer: Desire can serve as a cause of later moments of desire, and those later moments of desire are instances of desire that are effects of the previous cause.

Question: If a predisposition toward an action has formed in one's mind, must one inevitably complete it or is there a way out?

Answer: If you are able to bring about a condition that is more powerful than the condition that would cause that karma to manifest, it can be overwhelmed. For instance, through disclosing ill deeds, developing contrition, and engaging in virtuous activity aimed at purifying a bad karma, you can purify it. At minimum, you can diminish its force such that, even if you meet with a condition that would have caused it to become activated, it will not.

Life Impelled by Ignorance

CONDITIONS FOR SUFFERING

L ET US CONTINUE the description of the twelve links of dependent-arising. The fifth link is the six sense spheres—the inner promoters of consciousness, which are the eye, ear, nose, tongue, body, and mental senses. They are depicted in the painting by an empty house because the organs are developing but not yet functioning. That is, like an empty house, the externals required for functioning sense consciousnesses are developing, but internally, they are not yet functioning.

After this, there comes contact, the sixth link. Contact itself is a mental factor that distinguishes objects as pleasurable, painful, or neutral upon the coming together of object, sense power, and consciousness. The objects are visible forms, sounds, odors, tastes, tangible objects, and other phenomena not included in those five; the sense powers are the six organs—eye, ear, nose, tongue, body, and mental sense powers. When an object, a sense power, and a former moment of consciousness acting as an immediately preceding condition are present, a consciousness is generated, and the mental factor of contact distinguishes the object as pleasurable, painful, or neutral.

In general, a consciousness is produced by way of having three conditions. The first is called the observed-object condition;[21] this is an object that causes to be generated a consciousness having the object's own aspect. The second is the dominant condition,[22] a sense power that causes a particular consciousness to be able to apprehend only its respective type of object but not another type, as when the eye sense power gives a consciousness the capacity to apprehend visual objects but not sounds. The fact that a consciousness is produced as an experiential entity is due to an immediately preceding consciousness; this is the third condition, called the immediately preceding condition.[23]

Because it involves a meeting with an object and distinguishing it, contact is symbolized by a kiss. Contact takes place immediately prior to the production of feeling.

The seventh link of dependent-arising, feeling, is posited as a mental factor that experiences pleasure, pain, or neutral feeling once the object has been determined to be pleasurable, painful, or neutral by contact. According to one system of interpretation, feeling can range anywhere from the initial experience of pleasure or pain through to the pleasure of orgasm. Feeling is depicted as an eye pierced by an arrow. The eye is so sensitive that even a very small condition will cause a great deal of feeling. No matter what kind of feeling we have, pleasurable or painful, we cannot stay still with it—it is very effective, it drives us. Pleasurable feeling generates a strong drive for more, and pain generates a strong drive to avoid.

The eighth and ninth links, attachment and grasping, are both types of desire. The difference between them is that attachment is weaker than grasping. There are various divisions of attachment; for instance, desirous attachment is associated with the desire realm; attachment to destruction is a wish to be separated from painful feeling; and attachment to the form and formless realms is called attachment to mundane existence.

Attachment is depicted as a person drinking beer. This is easy to understand, is it not? No matter that you realize that it makes you fat and you do not want to be fat, you still keep drinking and drinking and drinking it. Attachment is a mental factor that increases desire, without providing any satisfaction.

Grasping, mentally grabbing at an object that one desires, is depicted by a monkey taking fruit. There are four varieties of grasping—at desired objects, at views of self, at bad systems of ethics and conduct, and at any of the remaining types of bad views. Such forms of grasping can be described in terms of both ordinary householders and those who have left the householder life and, though celibate, have an erroneous view. There are, however, more types of grasping than the four described here. For instance, if a person (1) has become temporarily free from desire with respect to the desire realm and (2) has a correct view, but (3) seeks to be reborn in a form or formless realm, he or she must accumulate a karma that will impel rebirth in that realm and hence is necessarily grasping for that type of life. Since the four types of grasping do not include such examples, they are not exhaustive. The list, therefore, is said to have been formulated only in order to overcome wrong ideas, not to be exhaustive.

In dependence upon name and form, sense spheres, contact, and feeling, one generates attachment to remaining with a pleasurable object and attachment seeking separation from a painful object. When such attachment is produced over and over again in stronger form, this constitutes grasping at desired sense-objects, such as pleasant forms, pleasant sounds, pleasant odors, pleasant tastes, and pleasant tangible objects. Such attachment and grasping serve to further potentialize or charge up the karmic potency established in the consciousness by a prior action motivated by ignorance. This causes the attainment of a new life-system in the desire realm. When that karma, the predisposition established in the mind, is nourished by attachment and grasping and becomes fully capable of producing the next lifetime, it is called "existence," the tenth link. Here the cause, the fully potentialized karma, is given the name of the effect, a new existence in the cyclic round of suffering. In the Consequence School, "existence" most likely refers to a fully potentialized state of the destructedness of an action, which itself is a functioning thing that will produce the next lifetime.

The picture of this tenth link is of a pregnant woman. At this point the karma that will produce the next lifetime is fully potentialized, though not yet manifest; analogously, a woman late in pregnancy has a fully developed child inside her womb that has not yet emerged. The tenth link lasts from the time of the fully potentialized karma up to the beginning of the next lifetime. Within it there are two divisions according to time—one level called "directional"[24] since it is directed toward going to the next lifetime, and another level called "in process"[25] since it refers to the potentialized karma at the time of the intermediate state between the two lifetimes.

The eleventh link is the dependent-arising of birth, depicted by a woman giving birth. The child in the womb of the pregnant woman in the previous picture is now changing its state.

The twelfth link is the dependent-arising of aging and death. There are two types of aging; the first is called "progressive" since from the moment of conception one is always aging; it occurs in every moment of life. The other type is called "deterioration," the usual degeneration of old age.

After aging comes death. Between these, there are cries of sorrow and many types of suffering, such as seeking but not getting what you want, getting what you do not want, and so forth.

IGNORANCE AS THE ROOT OF SUFFERING

Our lives begin with the suffering of birth and end with the suffering of death; between these two, there are many different consequences of aging and many unfortunate events. This is suffering, the first of the four noble truths, which we do not want—the problem we want to overcome. It is important to investigate whether there is any way to surmount such suffering or not. To understand this, it is necessary to investigate the causes of our situation. This is the relevance of the entire explanation of the twelve links of dependent-arising, beginning with the stage of ignorance.

When we examine any type of suffering now being experienced, we find that its root is ignorance. As long as we have ignorance, in any and every minute we can initiate an action that will serve as a cause for another rebirth. Through this process, we have already deposited limitless predispositions in our one stream of consciousness, potencies established by actions motivated by ignorance; we have a limitless number of such potentialities for future lifetimes in our consciousness right now.

We have been considering the twelve links of dependent-arising in terms of one round beginning with ignorance. In this context we can see that other rounds of dependent-arising are operating simultaneously since other instances of ignorance induce additional series. Also, one round of dependent-arising requires intersection with other rounds. For example, ignorance, action, and consciousness impel the force producing the next lifetime, but the eighth, ninth, and tenth links—attachment, grasping, and existence—must occur between consciousness and name and form in order to enable consciousness to produce the lifetime indicated by the fourth link, name and form. Also, since the tenth link, existence, represents the fully potentialized karma leading to birth, at the time of that particular birth another set of name and form, sense spheres, contact, and feeling will be operating. Again, the attachment, grasping, and existence that must come between links three and four must be preceded by their own respective name and form, sense spheres, contact, and feeling—links four, five, six, and seven; thus, there is another round of dependent-arising involved in their production. Hence, a single round of dependent-arising necessarily involves other rounds.

Since the first of the twelve links is ignorance and the last is aging and death, there might appear to be a beginning and an end, but since not one but many sets operate together, there is no end unless ignorance is removed. Until ignorance is overcome, there is nothing one can really do to end this process.

If we consider the twelve links of dependent-arising related with a lifetime in a bad transmigration as an animal, hungry ghost, or hell-being, in a former life there was a basic ignorance—obscuration with respect to the mode of being of phenomena—and in addition there was also an ignorance with respect to the relation between actions and their effects. These two were the motivating force, producing a nonvirtuous action that deposited a potency in the consciousness. This potency then served as the projecting cause of a life in a bad transmigration. The projecting cause was actualized or charged up by attachment and grasping, becoming fully potentialized as existence. The projected effects (effect-consciousness, name and form, sense spheres, contact, and feeling) and actualized effects (birth and aging/death) of suffering in a bad transmigration are produced in this way.

If we consider the twelve links of dependent-arising related with a lifetime in a good transmigration as a human, god, or demigod, the basic ignorance is the same—obscuration with respect to the mode of being of phenomena—but the action that is motivated by it is a virtuous action beneficial to others, such as abandoning killing. Such a virtuous action deposits in the cause-consciousness a good potency for rebirth in a lifetime of high status. This projecting cause was actualized or charged up by attachment and grasping such that it became fully potentialized as existence, whereupon it produced the projected and actualized effects of a lifetime in a condition of high status.

Reflecting in this same way on how others travel in cyclic existence serves as a technique for increasing compassion. Thus, vast methods of meditation are set forth both in terms of reflecting on these twelve links of dependent-arising in *oneself,* whereby a wish to leave cyclic existence is developed, and in terms of reflecting on these twelve links of dependent-arising in *others,* whereby compassion increases.

That completes our discussion of dependent-arising as the process of developing a lifetime in cyclic existence.

DEPENDENT-ARISING AS DEPENDENT IMPUTATION

Another mode of dependent-arising is the establishment of phenomena in dependence upon their parts. Any and all objects have parts. Physical objects have directional parts, and formless phenomena such as consciousness have temporal parts—earlier and later moments that form their continuum. If there were any such thing as a partless particle to serve as the building-block of a larger object, one could not discriminate between, for instance, its left and right sides or front and back. If the sides could not be discriminated, then no matter how many of them were assembled, one would not find anything more than the size of the original one. It would be impossible for them to amass. However, it is a fact that gross objects are produced through the coming together of many minute particles; thus, no matter how small the particle is, it must have directional parts, and through this logic it is established that there are no physical objects that are partless.

Similarly, with respect to a continuum, if the smallest moments of a continuum did not have earlier and later parts themselves, there would not be any possibility of their coming together to form a continuum. If a moment had no parts able to be in contact with what precedes and with what follows, there would be no way for such partless moments to form a continuum. Similarly, with respect to unchanging phenomena such as uncompounded space, there are parts or factors such as space in the eastern quarter and space in the western quarter or the part associated with this object and the part associated with that object. Thus every object, whether it is impermanent or permanent, changing or unchanging, has parts.

However, when the whole and parts of any particular object—the latter being that, in dependence upon which the whole is imputed—appear to our minds, the whole appears to have its own separate entity and the parts appear to be *its* parts. Is this not the case? Though they depend on each other, they seem to be their own entities.

Thus, there is a discrepancy between the way whole and parts appear and the way they actually exist, in that they seem to be their own separate entities but actually are not. However, this does not mean there are no objects that are wholes, because if there were no wholes, we could not speak of something as being a part of anything, for a whole is that in relation to which something is posited as its part. Hence, there are wholes, but their mode of existence is that they are designated in dependence upon their parts—they do not exist in any other way. This applies not just to changing, impermanent phenomena but also to permanent, unchanging phenomena and thus is broader in meaning than the former interpretation of dependent-arising, which is limited to phenomena arisen in dependence upon causes and conditions.

Analytical Unfindability

Dependent-arising has a profound implication. It connotes that if one is not satisfied with the mere appearance of an object but seeks, through extended analysis, the actual object to which the imputation is affixed, one does not come up with anything among or separate from the bases of imputation of that object that can be said to be the object. Take the self, or I, as an example: the I is the controller, or user, of mind and body, and the mind and body are the objects of use of that I. The I, body, and mind definitely do exist, and it cannot be denied that they perform their respective functions. The I is like an owner, and the body and mind belong to it. Indeed, we say, "Today there is something wrong with my body; therefore, I am tired." Or, "Today my body is fit; so I am very fresh." Such statements are valid, but with respect to one's arm, for instance, nobody says, "This is I," but still when one's arm is painful, we definitely do say, "I am in pain; I am not well." Despite this, it is clear that the I and the body are different; the body is something that belongs to the I.

Similarly, we speak of "my mind" or "my consciousness," as when we feel, "My memory is so poor; something is wrong." We can even seem to oppose our own consciousness, our own memory; is it not so? We say such things as, "I want to improve the sharpness of my mind; I want to train my mind," in which case the mind is both the trainer and the object trained. When the mind is unruly—not doing what one wants it to—one is like the teacher or trainer of the mind and the mind is like the unruly student that must be trained into obedience. We say and think such things, and they accord with the facts.

In this way, both body and mind are things that belong to the I, and the I is the owner; but, aside from mind and body, there is no separate, independent entity of I. There is every indication that the I exists; yet, under investigation, it cannot be found. For example, the Dalai Lama's I must be located within the confines of this area circumscribed by my body; there is no other place it could possibly be found. This is certain. However, if one investigates within this area what the true Dalai Lama, the true Tenzin Gyatso, is, besides this body and mind, the I does not have its own substance. Still, the Dalai Lama is a fact, a man, a monk, a Tibetan, someone who can speak, who can drink, who can sleep, who can enjoy life; is it not so? This is sufficient to prove that something exists, even though it cannot be found.

This means that among the bases of imputation of the I there is nothing to be found that is an illustration of the I or that is the I. Does this mean the I does not exist? No, it does not mean this; the I definitely does exist. But when it still cannot be found among its bases of imputation that constitute the place where it must exist, one has to say that it is established not under its own power but through the force of other conditions. It cannot be posited any other way.

Among the conditions in dependence upon which the I exists, one of the more important factors is the conceptuality that designates it. Thus it is said that the I and other phenomena exist through the power of conceptuality. In this way, dependent-arising comes to mean not just "arisen in dependence upon causes and conditions" or "imputed in dependence upon a basis of imputation" but also "arisen or imputed in dependence upon a conceptual consciousness that imputes the object."

Thus in the term "dependent-arising," "dependent"[26] means depending, or relying, on other factors. Once the object depends on something else, it is devoid of being under its own power—it is devoid of independence. Nevertheless, it does arise in reliance upon conditions. Good and bad, cause and effect, oneself and others—all objects are established in reliance upon other factors; they arise dependently. Due to being dependently arisen, objects are devoid of the extreme of being under their own power. Also, because, in this context of dependence, help and harm arise and exist, objects do not *not* exist—their performance of functions is feasible. In this way, the causes and effects of actions are feasible, as is the I that is the basis of them. When one understands this, one is released from the extreme view of non-existence, nihilism.

In this way, existing in dependence upon conceptuality is also a meaning of dependent-arising—the most subtle meaning. Nowadays, physicists explain that phenomena do not exist merely objectively in and of themselves but exist in terms of, or in the context of, involvement with a perceiver, an observer.

I feel that the topic of the relation between matter and consciousness is a place where Eastern philosophy—particularly Buddhist philosophy—and Western science could meet. I think that this would be a happy marriage, with no divorce! If we work along the lines of a joint effort by Buddhist scholars—not mere scholars but those who also have some experience in meditation—and pure, unbiased physicists to investigate, study, and engage in deeper research in the field of the relation between matter and consciousness, we may find beautiful things that may be helpful. This does not have to be considered the practice of religion but can be done simply for the extension of human knowledge.

Also, those scientists who are working on the human brain in the field of neurology could benefit from Buddhist explanations about consciousness—how it functions, how it changes in terms of levels, and so forth. Some time ago, I asked a neurologist how memory functions. He reported that they still had not found a concrete explanation; so, in this field, too, I think that we could work together. Some Western medical professionals are also showing interest in the curing of certain illnesses through meditation. This is another interesting topic for a joint project.[27]

Because of Buddhism's emphasis on self-creation, there is no creator-deity, and thus some people consider it, strictly speaking, not to be a religion. A Western Buddhist scholar told me, "Buddhism is not a religion; it is a kind of science of mind." In this sense, Buddhism does not belong to the category of religion. I consider this to be unfortunate, but in some sense it means that Buddhism becomes closer to science. However, from the pure scientist's viewpoint, Buddhism is a type of spiritual path. It is unfortunate that we do not seem to belong to the category of science either. Buddhism thereby belongs to neither religion nor pure science, but this situation provides us with an opportunity to make a link, or a bridge, between faith and science. This is why I believe that in the future we will have to work at bringing these two forces more closely together than they are at present.

The majority of people simply ignore religion. But among those who do not, there is, on the one side, a group who are following faith and experiencing the value of a spiritual path, and on the other side is a group who are deliberately denying any value to religion. As a result, there is constant conflict between these two factions. If, one way or another, we could help bring these two forces closer, it would be worthwhile.

QUESTIONS

Question: Your Holiness, would you please clarify the difference between actions of intention and intended actions?

Answer: With regard to actions, or karma, in general, there are two different systems—one that explains that any sort of karma is necessarily the mental factor of intention, and another that says that there are also physical and verbal karmas. According to the first system, the mental factor of intention itself, at the time when it is initially motivating an action, is called an action of intention, whereas the mental factor of intention at the time of actually engaging in the deed is called an intended action; thus, both are encompassed within the mental factor of intention. According to the system that posits that there are also physical and verbal actions, actions of intention are explained similarly, but intended actions occur at the point when the action is displayed physically or verbally, and thus intended actions can be either mental, physical, or verbal. The latter is a more preferable system; it is the assertion of the Consequence School.

Question: Regarding consciousness, it was said that in the Middle Way School, as opposed to the Mind Only School, the continual basis of a predisposition caused by an action is the mere I, while the temporary basis was said to be consciousness. Could you explain this further. Specifically, how can the everlasting basis of the predisposition be the mere I, which does not exist inherently or everlastingly? Also, how or what is the mechanism that stores the predisposition, since it is not the mind-basis-of-all, and how does it travel from one lifetime to the next?

Answer: When we speak of the nominally existent I that is a mere name, this does not mean that there is no meaning to I, or self, other than just the name. There is a meaning to which the name I refers. However, because the object I does not exist in a self-instituting way under its own power without depending on that name but exists depending very much on the name, on conceptual imputation, it is said that it is "name only"—merely nominally imputed. Thus, in the term "mere I," the word "mere" indicates that when the I is sought under analysis, it cannot be found. Not only is the I—which is the basis into which these predispositions are infused—merely nominally imputed, but also predispositions themselves as well as the actions that infuse the predispositions are nominally imputed, as is everything else. That phenomena are merely nominal does not mean that they do not exist at all; rather, it means that within existing, they do not exist under their own power, by way of their own entity, by way of their own character.

When it is said that the basis of infusion and of carrying the predispositions is "name-only," it might appear to your mind that then the basis of infusion really would not be much of anything. However, through this explanation you can understand that this is not the case and that there is no such difficulty. With regard to the means connecting a karma with its effect, consider this: In our conventional vocabulary we say, "At an earlier time I did such and such," and it is a fact that the agent of that action is oneself. From the viewpoint that oneself is a continuation of the mere I that performed the action, we say this, but if we look into the matter, the action has ceased, and the I of the present moment is not the I of the previous moment. Still, innately we have the thought and indeed say, "I did that," and this accords with the fact. One is, therefore, the owner of that action. In this way, there is a connection between the action and oneself, and this is what connects forward to the future effect of that action, no matter how much time passes. Since, for a person who performed an action and thereby accumulated the karma, the continuum of the mere I keeps going, one continues to be the I who accumulated that karma; since the action that was done earlier has to fructify, there is no one else for whom it can fructify except oneself.

The I is designated in dependence upon the mental and physical aggregates, and in terms of the tantric, or mantric, system there are coarse and subtle levels of those mental and physical aggregates. From the viewpoint of highest yoga tantra, the final basis of imputation of the I has to be a subtle aggregate that has been together with oneself since beginningless time; this is a subtle level of consciousness, the continuum of which is beginningless and uninterrupted, eventually reaching fulfillment in buddhahood. There is no question about whether afflicted minds go on to buddhahood—of course they do not. Even the coarser levels of consciousness do not; it is only the most subtle level of consciousness that proceeds to buddhahood. This subtle level has lasted since beginningless time and continues forever. When we die, our coarser levels of consciousness dissolve. On our last day, at the time of our death, the final consciousness that manifests is this most subtle mind of clear light; it is this consciousness that makes the connection to the next lifetime. In this way, the subtler aggregates necessarily exist continuously throughout time.

According to the Consequence School, when an action ceases or disintegrates, that disintegration is something that is caused; thus the state of having disintegrated that occurs after disintegration is also something that is caused—it is a produced phenomenon. The action establishes a state of destructedness that itself is an impermanent phenomenon, continuing until the time of the fruition of the karma and producing the fruition.

With regard to the way in which the I appears, there is a general type of I that has existed since beginningless time right through to the present, but with regard to particular I's, there is an I qualified, for instance, by one's own youth, and there is an I qualified by being related to a human lifetime as distinct from another type of life, and so on. For instance, we refer to the I of our own youth, "Oh, I used to be such a rascal when I was young, but nowadays I have improved a bit." Many such distinctions are to be made within the I, some general and pervasive and others more individual and less pervasive.

Question: Is material energy the same as mental energy?

Answer: In general, because matter and consciousness are different, it seems that the energy associated with them would be different.

With respect to mental energy, there are many grosser and subtler levels of consciousness; the grosser a level of consciousness is, the more it is related to the present body, whereas the subtler a consciousness is, the less connection it has with the gross physical body. Also, the subtler levels of mind are more powerful than the grosser levels; thus if one is able to utilize them, they are more effective for mental transformation. In order to discuss differences of energy, one has to consider many different levels of matter and consciousness.

Question: How can we abandon innate ignorance?

Answer: Certain types of ignorance can be removed with little exertion, but the type of ignorance that is the root of cyclic existence can only be removed with tremendous exertion. Indeed, the main topic of this series of lectures is how to bring about an end to ignorance. So far, I have been speaking about the basis, the foundation of one's practices. Next I will discuss the levels of practice.

Question: What is the most skillful way of dealing with anger and aggression without either submitting to the aggressor or becoming angry and aggressive oneself?

Answer: If you just keep letting anger out and expressing it, it is very difficult for this to be helpful. Since this behavior itself promotes more anger, it will not bring about any positive result; it will only increase problems. Under certain circumstances it may be necessary to take a counteraction to stop another's wrongdoing, but I believe that such measures can be enacted without anger. In fact, without anger, the implementation of countermeasures is much more effective than when your main mind is governed by a strong afflictive emotion, because under such influence you may not take the *appropriate* action. Anger destroys one of the best qualities of the human brain—judgment, the capacity to think, "This is wrong," and to investigate what the temporary and longterm consequences of an action will be. It is necessary to calculate such circumstances before taking action; free of anger, the power of judgment is better.

It is clear that if in a competitive society you are sincere and honest, in some circumstances people may take advantage of you. If you let someone do so, he or she will be engaging in an unsuitable action and accumulating bad karma that will harm him- or herself in the future. Thus it is permissible, with an altruistic motivation, to take a counteraction in order to help the other person avoid the effects of this wrong action in the future. For instance, wise parents, without any anger, may sometimes scold or even punish their children. This is permissible, but if the parent really gets angry and whacks the child too hard, then the parent will feel regret in the future. However, with a good motivation of seeking to correct a child's bad behavior, it is possible to respond in a way that is appropriate to what the child needs at that moment. Responses should be made in that way.

According to the sūtra system, the use of anger is not permitted in the spiritual path; however, within the tantric system there is an explanation that it is possible to utilize anger in the path. In this case, the fundamental motivation must be compassion, but the temporary motivation is anger, and the purpose is to utilize the strength and swiftness of anger without coming under its negative influence, so that practice becomes more effective.

Question: Is it better to leave hatred alone as a potential within oneself or to actualize it and thereby face it?

Answer: There is a practice in which in order to identify hatred—how the hated object appears, how one's mind reacts, what the nature of hatred is, and so forth—one allows the mind to generate hatred and then watches it, but this is not a case of displaying hatred externally and fighting with another person. If there is a danger of your going outside with an angry attitude, it is better to lock your door—with you inside—and then generate anger and examine it!

For certain types of mental problems, such as depression[28] and some other mental crises, it can be helpful to let them out by talking about them; this reduces the uncomfortable inner feeling. For other kinds of mental crises, such as anger or strong attachment, the more you express them, the more they will occur; with these types, restraint will cause them to weaken. However, restraint does not just mean that when you develop anger or attachment to a high degree, you attempt at that moment to control it, for that is very difficult. Rather, in daily practice you should continuously reflect on the benefits and advantages of compassion, love, kindness, and so forth and reflect on the disadvantages—the faults—of anger. Such continuous thoughtful contemplation and development of appreciation for compassion and love, whereby one continuously revives and increases such appreciation, has the effect of creating dislike for hatred and respect for love. Through the force of this, even when you become angry, the anger's expression changes in aspect and diminishes in force. This is the way to practice; as time passes, mental attitudes can gradually change.

Question: How is it possible for me to make an effort in my meditation practice when there is no me, no I?

Answer: Most likely, this is the misunderstanding I mentioned earlier: wrongly interpreting the emptiness of inherent existence as an emptiness of existence itself, such that it seems that nothing exists. This is wrong. If you think you do not exist, then stick a pin in your finger! Even if you cannot identify the I, that it exists is clear.

Question: I have received many teachings and initiations from my guru, but now I have lost some faith in him. What shall I do?

Answer: This is a sign of your not having been careful at the beginning. If faith alone were sufficient, there would have been no reason for the Buddha to have set forth the qualifications of a guru in great detail in explanations in the discipline, the sets of discourses, and secret mantra. It is said to be *very* important for both the guru, or lama, and the student to investigate each other. Still, this situation about which you are speaking does indeed occur; we should take such experiences as warnings and realize that we need a sounder basis—it is important to analyze, to investigate. I usually tell people that at the beginning, when receiving teachings, it is not necessary to regard the teacher as one's guru; rather, simply consider the teacher to be a religious friend from whom you are receiving teachings. Then if, as time passes, you examine the person's qualifications and gain real conviction, you can regard him or her as your own guru. This is a good procedure.

Now, to address your question about what to do: If the situation is that you first had faith and now you cannot generate faith, rather than coming to dislike the person, it would be better to develop a neutral attitude. Another helpful technique is to reflect on the fact that in Buddhism, and particularly in the Great Vehicle, even our enemy is considered to be one of the best gurus. Even though an enemy may *deliberately* harm you, it is a basic practice to develop deep respect and a feeling of gratitude toward that person. If that is the case, then it is even more so here, since your guru is most likely not deliberately harming you. It can help your mental attitude to look at the situation this way.

Question: What is your opinion about Western students of Buddhism doing the practice of protector-deities?

Answer: This is a complicated matter. Whether one practices religion or not is one's own decision, and what one does individually is one's own business. However, it is important to understand the context of such a practice. When we look into the history of this tradition, we find that the theory of protector-deities comes from tantric practice. In the sūtra systems, aside from an occasional mention of the four great royal kings, there is no mention of deities other than the likes of Mañjushrī, Avalokiteshvara, Tārā, Maitreya, and Samantabhadra. In Maitreya's *Ornament for Clear Realization,* at the point of the serial training in the six mindfulnesses, there is a practice of mindfulnesses of gods or deities, and indeed it might be possible that these latter deities as well as the great four kings appear within this practice. However, the context there is of being mindful of them as witnesses of your own actions.

On the other hand, *many* tantric texts mention protector-deities. In the tantric systems, a practitioner of a protector-deity first must gain initiation and then attain a deep state of meditation in which visualization practices of deity yoga eventually make one qualified to conduct this practice. While imagining oneself as a deity in a mandala, one visualizes a protector-deity in front of oneself and gives him or her an order that has a use in a particular field of action. Hence, if you want to engage in the practice of a protector-deity, you yourself must first be qualified.

In the past in Tibet, many people did the opposite, completely neglecting their own practice and simply running after protector-deities. This is absolutely wrong. One is supposed to achieve clear appearance of oneself as a divine figure within a full sense of being that deity, whereupon the protector comes under one's control; the practice is not at all a matter of the protector controlling oneself.

In fact, the best protector is Buddha, his doctrine, and the spiritual community. In a deeper sense, the actual protector and the actual destroyer are your own karma. If you ask what really helps, it is your own virtuous actions. If you ask what really harms, it is your own nonvirtuous actions. This is important.

Question: Must desire always lead to attachment?

Answer: In Tibetan there is a clear distinction between 'dod pa and 'dod chags; the first means desire, wishing, or wanting, which can either be reasonable or not, whereas the second is necessarily an afflictive emotion. Reasoned desire exists even in the continuum of a foe destroyer,[29] someone who has gone beyond cyclic existence. Despite this verbal difference, during the initial stages of practice when one is still a common being, it is difficult to distinguish between mere desire and afflictive desire, and one could even have faith that is mixed with the conception of inherent existence, or compassion that is mixed with the conception of inherent existence, in which oneself and the object of faith, or of compassion, are wrongly thought to be established by way of their own character. It is difficult to distinguish between these at the beginning, but through sustaining basic practice one can gradually identify the factors of ignorance and the afflictive emotions, thereby making practice more and more pure.

Levels of the Path

THE PATH

T HE TWELVE LINKS of dependent-arising of a lifetime in cyclic existence represent our basic situation—afflictive emotions, contaminated actions, and suffering. Can the mind be separated from such ignorance or not? This needs to be examined. Any type of consciousness we might consider is subject to conditioning, with familiarization. Still, no matter how much a mistaken consciousness increases in strength due to habituation, it cannot be increased limitlessly since it does not have a valid foundation certified by correct cognition. On the other hand, a consciousness with a valid foundation, even though it might not presently be very powerful due to one's not having become habituated to it, can always be strengthened through conditioning. Moreover, since it is validly founded, it eventually can become limitless.

It is said that mental qualities have a stable basis since consciousness, on which they are founded, has no beginning and no end. So long as one keeps practicing, one's mental qualities do not require the renewal of the exertion involved in first acquiring them, hence their strength can gradually be increased. Once a mental quality is in the mind with a certain force, one does not have to exert that degree of force again to bring it to that level; hence, additional training will increase that quality.

Since the root of suffering is ignorance, suffering stems from an untamed mind. Correspondingly, since relief from suffering comes from purifying and destroying the ignorance that is in the mind, it stems from taming the mind. Not taming the mind leads to suffering, whereas taming the mind leads to happiness. The mind is tamed by mental training. Since the trainer is a particular type of mind, and since that which is being trained is also the mind, one has to become skilled in psychology. Thus, in Buddhist texts a great deal of attention is devoted to the discussion of consciousness.

The most untamed type of mind—the grossest level of mind that apprehends its objects erroneously—is called *wrong knowledge*. Then, as the mind becomes accustomed to the teachings and so forth, it is transformed into the level of *doubt*. Within doubt there are three different levels; the lowest is doubt that tends toward what is wrong, the middle is equal doubt that tends toward both what is wrong and what is right, and the highest level is doubt that tends toward what is right. Through practice, doubt is gradually transformed into a level called *correctly assuming consciousness,* which, through continued training methods such as reflecting on reasons, turns into *inference.* Becoming accustomed to inferential understanding and developing an increasingly clear appearance of the object being understood, one attains *direct perception* of that object.[30]

In order to overcome wrong views that one-pointedly hold what is contrary to fact, one needs to reflect on the absurd consequences of such views. For this reason, Buddhist texts on logic present many forms of absurd consequences that break down the strength of adherence to wrong views. At the point at which one rises to the level of doubt, it is possible to make use of syllogistic reasonings aimed at generating an inferential understanding. This is why it is important to study the books of the two pillars of logic, Dignāga and Dharmakīrti, in order to develop and increase the wisdom of differentiating phenomena. In the process, a practitioner gradually generates the wisdom arisen from hearing, the wisdom arisen from thinking, and finally the wisdom arisen from meditation.

LEVELS OF PRACTICE

With this type of practice, one gradually comes to see that it is indeed possible to transform consciousness. From this perspective, one can develop conviction in the efficacy of the practice of nonviolence. The first level in the practice of nonviolence is to restrain oneself from engaging in activities that harm others; the second is to implement antidotes to afflictive emotions that drive bad actions, and the third is to overcome even the predispositions previously established by afflictive emotions. Reflecting on how the unwanted faults of cyclic existence stem from ignorance, one concludes that one must practice these three levels of nonviolence—first restraining the bad activities of the afflictive emotions, then restraining the afflictive emotions themselves, and finally restraining the predispositions established by afflictive emotions.

To remove latent predispositions, it is necessary first to extinguish the afflictive emotions, for without this there is no possibility of extricating the predispositions that they establish in the mind. The state of having entirely removed the afflictive emotions as well as their predispositions is called buddhahood, whereas the mere removal of the afflictive emotions is the stage of an *arhan*, a foe destroyer.

The destruction of the afflictive emotions and the predispositions established by them is much like an offensive engagement; thus, it is important to first engage in a defensive line of action, making sure that one will not come under the influence of any of these counterproductive emotions. This is why it is important initially to restrain ill deeds of body and speech. The final aim is the removal of all afflictive emotions together with their predispositions, that is, the attainment of buddhahood, but in implementing the means for bringing about this aim, one must initially prevent coming under the influence of ill deeds.

Restraining the Bad Activities of the Afflictive Emotions

When one acts with a selfish motive and commits wrong actions such as killing, stealing, adultery, lying, divisive talk, harsh speech, and senseless chatter, one not only harms others but also ultimately brings suffering on oneself. Thus, without even considering what violence does to others—considering only the violence inflicted on oneself in terms of the cause and effect of actions leading into cyclic existence—one can see that it is necessary to restrain ill deeds of body and speech. By thinking along these lines, one develops the conviction that harming others brings loss to oneself. This is to be reflected upon again and again.

It also is helpful to reflect on impermanence. No matter how long our life is, there is a limit to it, is there not? When we think about the formation of this universe and of geological time, the lifetime of a human is very short, and there is no guarantee that we can live out even a normal human lifespan. Under these circumstances, it is senseless to concentrate all one's energy, mental as well as physical, on accumulating money and property. Since it is very clear that wealth is helpful only for this life, it is appropriate to reduce extreme greed.

At this level of the teaching there is no reference to love and compassion for other people; rather, emphasis is on realizing that the ill deeds are detrimental even from the point of view of one's own welfare. Also, it is clear from the current world situation that no amount of material progress can fulfill what beings are seeking. Material progress alone does solve certain problems in some fields and sometimes develops new problems. Through our own experience we know that material progress is not sufficient on its own.

Again, at this stage, it is helpful to reflect on the usefulness of having gained the state of a human being. Considering how the human body can be utilized in a positive way, one understands that it is really sad to use it for a harmful purpose.

Also, for some people it is helpful to reflect on the sufferings of the three bad levels of transmigration: hell-beings, hungry ghosts, and animals. If it is difficult to believe that there are hell-beings, consider the many sufferings that animals undergo. With our own eyes we can see their manifold sufferings, but we should consider whether, born in that sort of situation, we would be able to stand such suffering. We can decide that we already have many predispositions in our minds established by non-meritorious actions—which were motivated by beginningless ignorance—that will result in rebirth as animals. Up to now, we have just looked at animals, but now we should imagine ourselves living as one of them; we should consider whether we could bear it or not. When we think in this way, we develop a sense of not wanting to be reborn as an animal. What brings about these results are acts of harmfulness and violence against others.

That is the first level of reflection on the faults of violence and the need to restrain ill deeds of body and speech. Still, there is no guarantee that even if one restrains such activities during this lifetime, one will not come under their influence in the next lifetime. Therefore, the best defense is to practice the next level of nonviolence, which can be called active engagement.

Restraining the Afflictive Emotions Themselves

The afflictive emotions that bring about all this trouble for us are those mentioned in the twelve links of dependent-arising. Their root is the ignorance that conceives objects as inherently existing; the force of this ignorance induces desire and hatred as well as many other types of afflictive emotion such as pride, doubt, enmity, jealousy, and so forth. These are real troublemakers. When we analyze the problems and crises of our present world, whether on the international level or in the family, it is clear that they are related to our anger, jealousy, and attachment.

Let us consider our so-called "enemy," whom we hate with strong feeling. Due to the fact that this person's mind is untamed, he or she engages in activities to bring injury to us, and it is because of this that we consider that person to be an enemy. If this anger—the wish to harm—were in the very nature of the person, it could not be altered in any way, but it is not the case that hatred subsides in the nature of that person. Rather, just like ourselves, the person displays bad behavior due to the influence of having generated an afflictive emotion. We ourselves engage in bad behavior, do we not? Still, we do not always think that we are completely bad. The situation is the same with this other person whom we consider to be an enemy. Consequently, the actual troublemaker is not the person but his or her afflictive emotion. The real enemy is an internal factor.

As practitioners, our real battle should take place within ourselves. It will take time, but this is the only way to minimize counterproductive human qualities. Through such practice, we will attain more mental peace, not only in the distant future of another lifetime but day-to-day.

In order to create peace of mind, the question of whether the afflictive emotions can be overcome is crucial. At this point, one is training to overcome the afflictive emotions, and to do this it is necessary to destroy their root, which is the ignorance that conceives inherent existence. To do this, it is necessary to generate a reasoning consciousness that perceives objects in exactly the opposite way to how we would perceive them with ignorance. Only such a consciousness can serve as an antidote to afflictive emotions.

Ignorance conceives phenomena to exist in and of themselves, whereas in fact objects do not exist this way; to overcome this ignorance it is necessary to refute with reasoning its conceived object—inherent existence. We must realize that objects do not exist inherently in and of themselves.

In order to develop a realization of emptiness capable of removing this ignorance, one cannot merely generate a reasoned inferential consciousness that realizes emptiness. In addition, one must bring this inferential understanding to the level of direct nonconceptual perception of the emptiness of inherent existence. In order to accomplish this, it is necessary to have the assistance of deep concentration, with which it is possible to develop *samādhi,* or meditative stabilization, a union of calm abiding and special insight. Thus it is said that in order to generate the wisdom-consciousness constituted by special insight into emptiness, it is necessary first to generate a calm abiding of the mind—a tranquilization and focusing of consciousness. It is advantageous to develop the mind's ability to remain on its object of observation in an alert and clear manner, and by developing vivid one-pointedness of mind, the mind gradually becomes more sharp, more alert, and more able. These are reasons for the detailed presentations of how to achieve meditative stabilization.

Someone who wants to achieve mental calm abiding cannot live as we do now but should stay in an isolated place, where continual practice can be cultivated over a long period of time. In addition, if one works at achieving calm abiding in connection with tantric practices, it is said to be easier. Still, for those not capable or ready for such intense practice, it is helpful to rise early in the morning and immediately use the mind—while it is still clear—to investigate the nature or entity of mind itself, without thinking about other topics. This practice helps to keep the mind alert, thereby helping one throughout the rest of the day.

In order to reach the point where even internal subtle distractions have been pacified and the mind remains vividly and continuously on its object of observation, one must first restrain grosser distractions, the coarse ill deeds of body and speech, that scatter the mind to objects of desire and hatred. For this, one needs training in ethics. The Buddhist system of ethics contains two levels—one for householders or lay persons, and one for those who have left the householder life. Even within the level of lay persons' ethics, there are several stages. So many variations occur because the Buddha set forth levels of practice in accordance with the varying capacities of individual people. It is crucial to follow a path according to one's own mental disposition; only then will one gain satisfactory results.

Because sentient beings have many and various dispositions and interests, the Buddha set forth many different levels of practice. Recognizing this is helpful not only in gaining a proper perspective on Buddhist teachings, but also in developing respect from the depths of the heart for the different types of religious systems that are present in this world, since they are all beneficial to those who believe in them. Even though the differences in philosophy are tremendous—often fundamental—still one can see that those philosophies are appropriate and beneficial in the conduct of people's lives, relative to their various interests and dispositions. Through understanding this, deep respect will be engendered. Today we need this kind of mutual respect and understanding.

Buddhism in the West

Quite a number of Western men and women have become monks and nuns. I respect their decision to take ordination, but there should be no rush to take vows. It needs to be remembered that since the Buddha set forth practices in accordance with various different levels of capacity, it is critical to determine what one's own level is and gradually to advance within that. It is important that those Westerners who sincerely want to practice Buddhism remain good citizens and members of society—remaining in their own communities without becoming isolated. It is important to adopt the *essence* of the Buddha's teaching, recognizing that Buddhism as it is practiced by Tibetans is influenced by Tibetan culture; it would be a mistake for Westerners to try to practice a Tibetanized form of Buddhism. Trying to completely Tibetanize their practice, Westerners may encounter difficulties, since such a system does not fit with their own minds and makes interaction with society difficult. Nowadays, some people act like Tibetans even to the point of keeping their heads down in an abject manner. Instead of copying such cultural forms, one should remain within one's own cul-

tural forms and implement the Buddha's teaching if something useful
and effective can be found in it. One should work in his or her profession as a member of the community. Although the various centers that
are already established are useful and should be maintained, it is not
necessary for someone who wants to practice Buddhism even to join
a particular center.

We have now discussed the first two levels of practice, of fighting
against afflictive emotions. Next we will consider the third level: how
to develop compassion in order to destroy the obstructions to omniscience, the predispositions established by afflictive emotions. Initially,
one trains in ethics, which forms the basis of all later practice; then,
through the practice of meditative stabilization the mind becomes
powerfully focused and effective in meditating on emptiness. Then
one eventually overcomes the obstructions to omniscience constituted
by the predispositions established by the conception of inherent existence. First, intellectually acquired obstructions are overcome, and
then gradually the innate obstructions are removed. Within innate
obstructions there are many levels of afflictive emotions to be overcome, but finally one completely extricates the ignorance that is the
root of all afflictive emotions—the conception of inherent existence.
This ignorance and all the afflictive emotions induced by it are extinguished, or pacified, in the sphere of reality. The wisdom that realizes
emptiness directly undermines the ignorance that conceives inherent
existence, and the extinguishing of that ignorance in the sphere of reality is called liberation. As the protector Nāgārjuna says in his *Treatise
on the Middle:*

> When actions and afflictive emotions cease,
>   there is liberation.
> Actions and afflictive emotions arise from false conceptions,
>   which in turn arise from fictive elaborations.
> Fictive elaborations cease in emptiness.[31]

Contaminated actions and afflictive emotions are produced from wrong conceptuality, which itself is produced from the elaborations of the conception of inherent existence. Those conceptual elaborations are ceased *through* emptiness,[32] or, those elaborations are ceased in emptiness[33]—the final line being interpreted in both of these ways. The former means that conceptual elaborations are ceased *through* cultivating the view that realizes emptiness. Because that into which they are extinguished is the reality of emptiness itself, here emptiness is also interpreted as that *into which* the fictive elaborations of the conception of inherent existence cease. That reality—the emptiness into which all of the afflictive emotions have been extinguished through the antidote of wisdom—is the true cessation of the sources of suffering: liberation.

QUESTIONS

Question: I have heard that becoming drowsy during meditation on the breath may indicate that this particular method is not a suitable practice and that one should seek an alternative method. Could you please comment on this.

Answer: It often happens that when people meditate, they become drowsy or even go to sleep; therefore, for some people with insomnia, I even advise them to recite mantra!

During meditation the mind can come under the influence of lethargy, a heaviness of mind and body that leads to drowsiness and even sleep. This is due to the fact that the mode of apprehension of the mind has become too loose; a counteractive technique is to make the mind more taut, whereby it is revitalized. If this does not work, then one should imagine something bright or pay attention to the details of the object being meditated upon, since lethargy is caused by the mind's being withdrawn too much inside. If this too does not work, one can leave the session and look far into the distance, perhaps at a panoramic view, or wash one's face, or go out into the fresh air.

If you become unusually sleepy when concentrating on the breath but do not experience this when concentrating on some other object, the problem may be a physical one. In that case, it might be suitable to switch your object. It might help to meditate on a certain element or a certain type of light at a particular channel-center. Also, it might be advisable, while contemplating the breath, to meditate on light in the upper part of the body. In general, it is said that when the mind sinks and becomes lax, it is helpful to move the object upward, and that when the mind becomes excited, it helps to move the object downward. The remedy has to be geared to the meditator's particular situation.

Question: What advice do you have for the parents of a seven-year-old child who has brain cancer? She is undergoing treatment in London at this moment.

Answer: No doubt the parents will use every means to bring about a cure medically. In addition, there are cases where it is helpful to employ meditative techniques such as repeating mantras and using certain visualizations, but whether these could be effective right away depends on a great many factors. In addition, in the Buddhist system, when one has tried other methods and those have not been effective, it is most beneficial to reflect on the inevitable cause and effect of actions—karma. Those who believe in a creator can think of such difficulties as being activities of God and gain comfort from this way of seeing things. The most important factor is that the small child must remain mentally peaceful. Beside these points, it is difficult to make suggestions. It is said that when the effect of an action is in the stage of manifest fruition, it is very difficult to reverse it.

Question: We are told that progress along the spiritual path depends upon faith. What is the substantial cause of faith?

Answer: In general, faith is of three types—the faith of clear delight, the faith of wishing to achieve a beneficial quality, and the faith of conviction. Concerning the main causes of faith, it is helpful to reflect on *reasons* that promote conviction and, beyond that, to develop actual *experience* yourself. As you think more and more upon reason, your ascertainment increases; this, in turn, induces experience, whereby faith becomes more firm.

Within faith and other types of spiritual experience, there are basically two types—one that comes by adventitious causes, suddenly sweeping over one, and another that comes by exerting effort over a long period of time. The latter is more stable, but adventitious experiences are nevertheless beneficial. It is helpful when you have a sudden, unusual, and profound experience, to take hold of it and sustain it with effort right at that time.

Question: I find it difficult to comprehend all the different levels of practice. What is a simple basic practice that I could bear in mind?

Answer: In brief, it is what I usually say: At best, if you are able to do so, then help others, and if you are not able to do so, at least do not harm others. This is the main practice. The essence of the teaching of the Vehicle of Hearers is to refrain from harming others; the essence of the teaching of the Great Vehicle is altruism—the helping of others. In terms of the stages of practice, on the first level one restrains ill deeds in the context of avoiding the ten nonvirtues and then takes vows relative to that level; later one performs more altruistic practices and takes vows related to this vaster level.

Question: Is it possible to reconcile special love for one person, as in

1. The wheel of cyclic existence in six sectors.

2. In the middle, the sources of suffering—ignorance (pig), desire (rooster), and hatred (snake)—surrounded by the good and bad actions motivated by them.

3. The sectors of gods and demi-gods.

4. The sectors of humans and gods.

5. The sector of animals.

6. The sector of hungry ghosts.

7. The sector of hell-beings.

marriage, with equanimity? Or is it only possible to develop equanimity if one is completely non-attached with no personal involvements?

Answer: During the initial stages of practice one has different levels of love—stronger for those who are, for the time being, closer to oneself and weaker for those who are not so close. However, as one practices and gradually develops, one's love becomes equal in strength toward each and every being. Such all-pervasive, equal love, however, cannot come right away; it must be developed gradually. As I was saying earlier, in the initial stages of practice love, compassion, faith, and so forth are mostly mixed with at least a little of the afflictive emotions.

Question: If a wholesome thought is followed by an unwholesome action, which has the greater karmic effect?

Answer: The effect depends both upon the type of action done at the point of executing the action and also upon the extent of one's motivation prior to engaging in the action—how vast it is in terms of the field of motivation. There are cases in which the motivation, because powerful and vast, comes to be stronger in effect, and other cases in which the actual execution of the action comes to be stronger due to the situation—the object and the time.

Question: Many Buddhists find it disturbing to hear of Buddhist teachers who regularly break certain precepts by, for example, saying that it is permissible to drink alcohol, to cohabit with members of the spiritual community, and so forth. Are there ever any circumstances under which these precepts may be broken?

Answer: It is said in the scriptures of the Bodhisattva Vehicle that for the maturation of one's own mental continuum there is the practice of the six perfections—giving, ethics, patience, effort, concentration, and wisdom—and for the maturation of others' continuums there are the four means of gathering students—giving material things to students; speaking pleasantly, which means to teach how to gain better lifetimes within cyclic existence and how eventually to leave cyclic existence; causing students to adopt in practice what is helpful and to discard from within their behavior what is counterproductive; and practicing oneself all of what one teaches others. Therefore, what one teaches others, one must also practice. With common sense we can see that it is not suitable to explain practices to other people and then do something else oneself. Speaking frankly, when what a person teaches and what that person practices are contradictory, it means that he or she does not have the full qualifications of a spiritual guide.

It is said that it is important for a student to understand the qualifications of a guru set forth in the Buddha's scriptures on discipline, in the discourses, and in tantra prior to making a religious connection with someone as his or her teacher and to analyze whether or not the person has these qualifications. Also, a person who wishes to become a lama teaching others must understand these qualifications and work at fulfilling them.

In the tantra system there is a procedure for great adepts, who are at a very high level of realization, to behave in unusual ways. The boundary line for engaging in these unusual activities is said to be when the adept has "attained capacity." What is the meaning of having attained capacity? The great Druk-ba Ga-gyu-ba scholar and adept Padma Gar-bo[34] said that this means that the yogi has reached the point whereby, through the power of yoga, he or she is capable of overcoming the non-faith that would be caused in others by the display of those activities. For instance, the great *paṇḍita* Tilopā, despite displaying many unusual modes of behavior to Nāropā, was fully capable of overcoming his non-faith. Thus, unusual deeds may be done only after having attained such capacity. On the other hand, if a lama who does not have such a capacity still tries to legitimate his or her irregular behavior, this just indicates that his or her back is to the wall.

Question: Would you please explain the nature of the connection between an action completed many lifetimes ago and its karmic result as experienced through a natural disaster, such as being struck by lightning? Is it that our present consciousness, or mindstream, affects or creates the lightning?

Answer: With respect to karma, it is relatively easy to understand through reasoned analysis that in general a virtuous action will lead to a pleasurable effect because of a similarity of nature between cause and effect. However, when one considers a specific action at a specific time that creates a specific effect at a specific time, these factors are extremely subtle and thus difficult to understand. With regard to the example of being hit by lightning, as I mentioned earlier there are four procedures for researching or investigating objects. One of them is to examine the nature of an object that is not created by karma but is just naturally so, as heat and burning are the very nature of fire and as wetness and moistening are the very nature of water. Similarly, lightning is produced through the machinations of the elements of this world system itself, but the fact that one was at the spot where the lightning hit—that one encountered this particular circumstance—is indeed due to karma. Many such distinctions have to be made.

Question: How can good Buddhists who are committed to not killing happily enjoy the results of murder by eating meat, fowl, and fish?

Answer: This is a real point. In general, in Buddhist scriptures on discipline, the eating of meat is not prohibited. Also, monks and nuns are persons who, in a sense, are mendicants going out and begging for food and thus do not, when begging, state a preference such as "I would like such and such kind of food." More than fifteen years ago, I discussed this matter with a Sri Lankan monk, who said that, strictly speaking, Buddhist monks and nuns are, therefore, neither necessarily vegetarian nor nonvegetarian.

In the Bodhisattva Vehicle, the general emphasis is on being vegetarian; not eating meat is mostly considered to be preferable, and indeed some Japanese Buddhist communities are strictly vegetarian. I think that this is the proper practice. Then, in the Tantra Vehicle, the three lower tantra sets—action, performance, and yoga—prohibit meat-eating, but in highest yoga tantra there is no prohibition against eating meat.

These are the general explanations offered by the scriptures on discipline, the Sūtra Vehicle, and the Mantra Vehicle. More specifically, it is unsuitable to have an animal killed for oneself. For example, in a market in a big city meat is already available to be bought and eaten, but in a place where no meat is available it is not suitable to say, "I want meat."

Still, the best way is to be vegetarian. I myself tried in 1965 to become a vegetarian, and remained so for twenty-two or twenty-three months. Then I contracted severe jaundice and was advised by my physician to discontinue vegetarianism. For those people who can follow strict vegetarianism, that is best. I was deeply impressed the other day when I heard on the BBC radio that the number of vegetarians in this country is growing. This is good news.

Question: You said that letting out anger was not a good practice. I assume you mean that it is not good to express anger to the person who is the object of the anger. However, some psychological systems advocate the expression of anger at a separate object, such as a pillow or a wall, to release the energy that resides in the angry person. Is this technique useful, or is it harmful?

Answer: In principle it is not at all good to express or let out hatred. Nevertheless, if you neglect to implement an antidote, such as cultivating patience and love, anger will increase. Thus, in principle it is better to try to minimize hatred. One of my friends says that when his anger becomes fully developed such that he feels intense irritation, he hits himself. I also think that this could be helpful. The questioner mentioned hitting a wall or pillow; I think a pillow is much better, because it will not be so hard! Under particular circumstances it seems permissible to let anger come out, but without harm to others.

Question: Several of us had to tell a few lies at work in order to be able to come here and benefit from your teaching. Is the bad karma acquired from telling lies countered by the good karma acquired through learning?

Answer: It depends on how much benefit is gained. If you implement the teachings in practice and thereby gain something for your way of life, then it is worthwhile. Whether it is beneficial depends on such factors. In Buddhism, as Shāntideva says, the most important considerations are the results of our actions; we have to distinguish what to do and what not to do in terms of determining what can be accomplished. In this context, activities that are completely prohibited in the scriptures on discipline are not only allowed but are required under certain circumstances—they *must* be done if they will be beneficial. Just as, in medical treatment, different medicines are used even by the same person under new circumstances, so when furthering the process of purifying the mind, different circumstances call for the implementation of different techniques.

The Value of Altruism

RESTRAINING THE PREDISPOSITIONS
ESTABLISHED BY AFFLICTIVE EMOTIONS

THE PRACTICE of the three trainings in ethics, meditative stabilization, and wisdom is capable of destroying the afflictive emotions; however, it is also necessary to get rid of the latent predispositions established by afflictive emotions, and this is extremely difficult. The reason for seeking to eradicate those predispositions is that they prevent simultaneous knowledge of all objects of knowledge. Even though persons who have achieved the state of a foe destroyer have extricated themselves from cyclic existence, they have not fully developed the potential of human consciousness—they are still only halfway on the path.

The question is *how* to destroy these predisposing tendencies. The actual weapon is the same—the wisdom that understands emptiness—but to overcome such latencies the powerful backing of great merit is needed. The technique for constantly accumulating great merit is unusual altruism. Until now, the main concern has been with this one being, oneself. In altruistic practice the concern is with *all* sentient beings.

Sentient beings are limitless; therefore, when one's consciousness is concerned with this infinite number of sentient beings, the meritorious power that is accumulated by virtuous activities is also limitless. Hence, going for refuge to the Buddha, the doctrine, and the spiritual community out of concern for oneself and going for refuge out of concern for a limitless number of sentient beings differ greatly in their meritorious power.

Also, until now, the aim has been to achieve mere liberation from cyclic existence—a mere extinguishment of suffering—for oneself; with the more altruistic motivation the aim is the highest possible attainment, buddhahood. This entails the extinction not just of the afflictive obstructions but also of their predispositions, which constitute the obstructions to omniscience. Thus, also from the viewpoint of the aim, or goal, the practices of the more altruistically motivated person seeking highest enlightenment will be more powerful, accumulating a greater meritorious force.

The nature of an altruistic mind is precious. It is indeed amazing that the human mind can develop such an attitude, for one forgets oneself and considers every other being to be as dear as oneself. That is truly marvelous. If someone shows us warm feeling, we feel very happy, and it is the same when we show *other* people sincere concern. I think that with such an attitude, all of cyclic existence would be like nirvana. This is the real source of happiness, not only in the long run, but even today. If even the slightest experience of this develops, it will help by bestowing peace of mind and inner strength. It attracts the best of all experiences and provides the best ground for active participation in society. It serves not only as a teacher but also as best friend and protector. It is truly good.

This morning we discussed the philosophical structure that allows us to conclude that it is possible to develop such a beautiful mind. The great Indian *paṇḍitas* set forth two techniques for the development of altruism—one through the seven quintessential instructions of cause and effect and the other through equalizing and switching self and other. The seven quintessential instructions of the former technique, preceded by a preliminary practice of developing equanimity with respect to all beings, are as follows: to (1) recognize all as friends, (2) reflect on their kindness, (3) develop an intention to repay that kindness, (4) generate love, (5) generate compassion, (6) develop the high resolve of universal responsibility, and (7) engender an altruistic intention to become enlightened.

In order to generate such a strong altruistic attitude in which one promises to seek buddhahood for the sake of others, it is necessary beforehand to generate an unusual resolve in which one takes on the burden of others' welfare. In order to induce this unusual resolve, it is necessary to have compassion in which one cannot bear to see either the manifest suffering of others or their oppression by unwanted internal conditions that result in suffering. Thus, from the depths of the heart one wishes that they be freed from such a condition. For, unless one is stirred from the depths by compassion, the high resolve in which one takes on the burden of freeing beings from suffering cannot be induced.

It is clear from our own experience that it is easier to generate compassion for other persons who are attractive to oneself or to whom one feels a sense of pleasantness—with whom one feels a sense of rapport. Thus prior to generating great compassion one needs a technique to cause all sentient beings to appear appealing and attractive to oneself. This technique involves viewing all sentient beings the way we already view those beings to whom you usually are the closest, whether these be our mother and father, relatives, or others.

In order to view beings this way, it is necessary first to see them in an even-minded way, and helpful here to use the imagination. Imagine in front of yourself a friend, an enemy, and someone to whom you are completely indifferent—a "neutral" person. Examine your feelings to see whom you hold dear and whom you consider in a distant manner. Naturally, you feel close to your friend; you feel not only distant but sometimes also angry or irritated toward your enemy; you just feel nothing for the neutral person. You have to investigate why this is so. The first one is your best friend; however, from the Buddhist viewpoint, although today he or she is acting like a friend, this is not permanent, because over the course of beginningless rebirths, in some past lifetime he or she may have been one of your worst enemies. Similarly, although the other one is today acting like an enemy, you cannot at all be sure that in a past life he or she was not one of your dearest friends.

In the future also, there is no reason why an enemy must always remain an enemy and a friend remain always a friend—there is no guarantee even within this life. Today's friend, within a short period of time, may change.

This is confirmed by our experience of life and, even more so, in political life—today one's ally, the next moment one's worst enemy! In this way, the basic life-structure is not at all stable: sometimes we are successful, sometimes unsuccessful; things are always changing, changing, changing. Therefore, our experience of such solid and stable feelings toward friends and enemies is absolutely wrong. There is no reason to assume such rigidity; it is foolish, is it not? Considering this will gradually help you to become even-minded.

The next step is to think that, given that your enemy was in the past—or will sooner or later be—a good friend, it is much better to consider all three persons as your best friends. Also, you can investigate whether there is value in showing hatred: what kind of result will come from it? The answer is obvious. However, if you try to develop compassion toward these persons, there is no question that the result will be nice. From this viewpoint also, you can see that it is much better to develop a compassionate attitude equally toward all three types of beings.

Extend this feeling toward your neighbors—one by one, to those living on this side and then to those on that side of the street. Then, to the whole country, then to the entire continent, then to all of humanity in this world, and then farther to infinite sentient beings. This is how to practice the seven quintessential instructions of cause and effect.

The other technique for developing altruism is called equalizing and switching self and other. Here, one should investigate which side is important, oneself or others. Choose. There is no other choice— only these two. Who is more important, you or others? Others are greater in number than you, who are just one; others are infinite. It is clear that neither wants suffering and both want happiness, and that both have every right to achieve happiness and to overcome suffering because both are sentient beings.

If we ask, "Why do I have the right to be happy?" the ultimate reason is, "Because I want happiness." There is no further reason. We have a natural and valid feeling of I, on the basis of which we want happiness. This alone is the valid foundation of our right to strive for happiness; it is a human right, and a right of all sentient beings. Now, if one has such a right to overcome suffering, then other sentient beings naturally have the same right. In addition, all sentient beings are basically endowed with the capacity to overcome suffering. The only difference is that oneself is single, whereas others are in the majority. Hence, the conclusion is clear; if even a small problem, a small suffering, befalls others, its range is infinite, whereas when something happens to oneself, it is limited to just one single person. When we view others as sentient beings too in this way, oneself seems not so important.

Let me describe how this is practiced in meditation. This is my own practice, and I frequently speak about it to others. Imagine that in front of you on one side is your old, selfish I and that on the other side is a group of poor, needy people. And you yourself are in the middle as a neutral person, a third party. Then, judge which is more important— whether you should join this selfish, self-centered, stupid person or these poor, needy, helpless people. If you have a human heart, naturally you will be drawn to the side of the needy beings.

This type of reflective contemplation will help in developing an altruistic attitude; you gradually will realize how bad selfish behavior is. You yourself, up to now, have been behaving this way, but now you realize how bad you were. Nobody wants to be a bad person; if someone says, "You are a bad person," we feel very angry. Why? The main reason is simply that we do not want to be bad. If we really do not want to be a bad person, then the means to avoid it is in our own hands. If we train in the behavior of a good person, we will become good. Nobody else has the right to put a person in the categories of good or bad; no one has that kind of power.

The ultimate source of peace in the family, the country, and the world is altruism—compassion and love. Contemplation of this fact also helps tremendously to develop altruism. Meditating on these techniques as much as possible engenders conviction, desire, and determination. When with such determination you try, try, try, day by day, month by month, year by year, we can improve ourselves. With altruistic motivation every action accumulates good virtues—the limitless power of salutary merit.

THE SIX PERFECTIONS

From a Buddhist viewpoint, what kind of help can we bring to others? One important type of charity is the giving of material things such as food, clothing, and shelter to others, but this is limited, for it does not bring complete satisfaction. Just as our own experience confirms that through gradual purification of our own mind more and more happiness develops, so it is the same for others; thus it is crucial that others understand what practices they should adopt in order to achieve happiness. To facilitate their learning these topics we need to be fully capable of teaching them. Moreover, since sentient beings have limitlessly different predispositions, interests, dormant potential, and attitudes, we cannot fulfill the hopes of other beings unless we develop the exalted activities of speech that accord exactly with what they need. There is no way to accomplish this unless we overcome the obstructions preventing omniscience in our own mental continuums. Thus, in seeking to help others we resolve to attain the stage of buddhahood in which the obstructions to omniscience have been extinguished.

In this way, the bodhisattva attitude is described as a mind intently directed toward the welfare of others, and aspiring to one's own buddhahood in order to accomplish this. Though the final aim is altruistic service upon the attainment of buddhahood, in terms of actual present implementation a bodhisattva engages in the practice of the six perfections—giving, ethics, patience, effort, concentration, and wisdom—in accordance with his or her capacity, beginning with the charity of giving material things.

Giving means to train from the depths of the heart in an attitude of generosity such that one seeks no reward or result for oneself; the act of charity and all of its beneficial results are dedicated to other sentient beings.

Concerning ethics, the root practice of a bodhisattva is to restrain self-centeredness. Since the practice of charity cannot involve any harm to others if it is to succeed, it is necessary to overcome the very root of any tendency to harm others. This must be done through eliminating self-centeredness, since a solely altruistic attitude leaves no room for harming others. Thus, the ethic of restraining self-centeredness is crucial.

In order to have pure ethics, it is necessary to cultivate patience. The practice of patience is extremely important since it is the main bulwark for training in the equalizing and switching of self and others. It is most helpful to practice together the techniques that Shāntideva sets forth in the chapters on patience and on concentration in his *A Guide to the Bodhisattva's Way of Life*,[35] in which he explains the equalizing and switching of self and others. The practice of patience establishes the foundation, the basis, for equalizing and switching self and others. It is hardest to generate a sense of affection and respect for enemies. When one thinks of enemies in terms of the practice of patience, not only is an enemy not someone who brings harm, an enemy is the most benevolent of helpers. One comes to think, "Without someone to harm me, there would be no way I could cultivate the patience of being unconcerned about harm to myself."

As Shāntideva says, there are many beings to whom one can practice charity, but there are very few beings with respect to whom one can practice patience, and what is more rare is more valuable. An enemy is really most kind. Through cultivating patience one's power of merit increases, and the practice of patience can only be done in dependence upon an enemy. For this reason, enemies are the main instigators of the increase of meritorious power. An enemy is not someone who prevents but in fact helps the practice of religion.

In his *A Guide to the Bodhisattva's Way of Life* Shāntideva states a hypothetical objection: "But an enemy does not have a motivation to help one and thus should not be respected." Shāntideva's answer is that for something to help it is not necessary that it have motivation. If motivation were necessary, there would be no way to have faith in the state of liberation from suffering. Thus even if enemies do not have a wish to help, it is suitable to respect them since they are beneficial.

Then, Shāntideva lodges a further hypothetical complaint: "Even if the state of liberation does not have a wish to help, it also does not want to harm; an enemy, however, wants to harm." Shāntideva's answer is: "Because a person has a wish to harm, that person gets the name 'enemy,' and you need an enemy in order to cultivate patience. Because a doctor, for instance, is seeking to help you, you do not identify him as an 'enemy' and hence he cannot provide a situation for the cultivation of patience." Such is the experience and reasoning of the great bodhisattvas of ancient times. Thinking along these lines is very beneficial. It helps one to remain happy. Shāntideva reasons that if something can be done to fix a situation, there is no *need* to worry, whereas on the other hand, if there is nothing that can be done, there is no *use* in worrying.

Another important type of patience is forbearance, the voluntary assumption of suffering.

Before suffering ensues, it is important to engage in techniques to avoid it, but once suffering has started, it should be regarded not as a burden but as something that can assist one. The reasons are many. Through undergoing small sufferings in this lifetime one can purify the karma of many ill deeds accumulated in former life-times. Also, suffering helps reveal the faults and disadvantages of cyclic existence: the more one can see the faults of cyclic existence, the more one will develop a dislike for engaging in nonvirtues. Suffering also helps reveal the good qualities and advantages of lib-eration. In addition, through your own experience of suffering you can infer what the pain of others is, and generate a wish to do something for them. Thinking about suffering in this way, one dis-covers that it provides a good opportunity for more practice and thought.

The fourth of the six perfections is effort. Of the many types of effort, one is called "putting on armor"; it prevents dissatisfaction with the lack of immediate achievement. Effort affords a willingness to engage in enthusiastic practice for eons and eons in order to bring about development.

QUESTIONS

Question: At the time of conception, does the consciousness mix with the developing physical aggregates, or can the consciousness join the physical body later, just a few moments before birth?

Answer: It is said that the consciousness enters at the time of concep-tion itself. To murder a human means to kill either a human or some-thing forming as a human, the latter referring to the period from right after conception until birth.

Question: Is abortion suitable when severe handicap has been detected in the embryo?

Answer: There might be situations in which, if the child will be so severely handicapped that it will undergo great suffering, abortion is permissible. In general, however, abortion involves the taking of life and is not appropriate. The main factor is motivation.

Question: What are the karmic consequences of a woman choosing to have an abortion while understanding that it is wrong to take life?

Answer: It is said that if there are no mitigating circumstances, it is worse to do an ill deed knowing that it is wrong.

Question: What advice can you give to those of us who have had an abortion but are currently practicing Buddhism?

Answer: When a wrong deed has already been done, then after learning that it was wrong, one can disclose the faulty deed [in the presence of actual or imagined holy beings] and develop an intention not to do that action again in the future. This diminishes the force of the ill deed.

Question: In the West there is a growing problem of drug and alcohol dependence. Do you have any advice as to how those afflicted can help themselves or be helped by those around them?

Answer: When drugs are taken, one's mind comes under the influence of additional delusion beyond that which we usually have. Double delusion is certainly not needed; what we require are techniques to relieve the basic situation. Knowing the nature of cyclic existence and training in altruism should help.

Question: Please say something about euthanasia, which can be performed either by withholding treatment or by giving an active drug that kills the person in a few minutes.

Answer: Again, there may be exceptional situations, but in general it is better to let persons die at their own time. What we undergo is due to our own past actions, and we have to accept what our karma has impelled us toward. Initially, we have to do whatever we can to avoid suffering, and then if nothing will relieve the problem, the suffering should be understood as the unavoidable result of former actions.

Question: Your Holiness, you talked about a subtle consciousness continuing as a stream from one lifetime to the next, but after liberation takes place, what happens to the stream of consciousness at the time of death? Does it continue?

Answer: The subtlest level of consciousness proceeds to and through buddhahood. It is never extinguished.

Question: Many of us so enjoy living that we cannot imagine wanting to escape it; thus, some aspects of Buddhist philosophy seem unduly depressing. Could you please comment?

Answer: From a Buddhist perspective, this is a case of not understanding the various levels of suffering. If you are truly happy, then it is okay!

Question: To what extent does the lack of a concept of a creator god prevent us as Buddhists from working and practicing alongside other religions?

Answer: Given the fact that sentient beings have such different dispositions and interests, there are beings for whom the theory of a creator god is suitable and helpful, and thus you should not make trouble for yourself worrying about working alongside such a person. A considerable number of people who believe in a creator god have reached a state without selfishness, and this proves that different teachings bring beneficial results. When we look at the results, respect for different religions grows.

Question: I have read about the Buddhist teaching of selflessness, which is often translated as "no soul." Yesterday you spoke about the subtlest continuum of consciousness as that which passes from one birth to another and is the inheritor of karma. Is there any essential difference between the subtle consciousness and the Christian concept of soul, leaving aside the question of reincarnation, which orthodox Christian teaching does not accept?

Answer: I wonder what a clear definition of soul is in Christianity. Since ancient times in India, there have been systems of tenets that assert a self, *ātman,* which is described as being permanent, unitary, and independent. This type of soul is not asserted in Buddhism.

Question: How can I overcome the strong fear of the unkind and hostile attitudes of others that I have experienced since childhood?

Answer: Cultivation of an attitude of cherishing others more than yourself will gradually help. It will take time. Also, if such a thought constantly causes discomfort for you, it would be better to try to stop thinking about it.

Question: What do you think of a Buddhist who does not believe in karma or rebirth?

Answer: This indeed needs to be considered. Generally, whether or not one is a Buddhist is determined by whether or not one asserts the Three Jewels—the Buddha, his doctrine, and the spiritual community—as pure sources of refuge. However, there are persons who do this without much thought on complicated matters such as former and later births, karma, and so forth. On the other hand, some Western people who think more along these lines cannot immediately accept the Three Jewels and remain skeptical, but nevertheless have high regard for the Buddha, his teaching, and the spiritual community. The latter, it might be said, are persons who are about to become Buddhists. Also, although Buddhists would not assert a permanent, unitary, independent self, there could be Buddhists who would not immediately accept selflessness.

Question: How is it possible to practice Buddhism while living among people—wife, husband, or family—who do not practice?

Answer: Buddhism is to be practiced individually; there is no necessity to recite texts together, for instance.

Question: What is your advice to an ordinary Westerner who is working but wants to complete Tibetan Buddhist practices without either becoming a monk or performing a three-year retreat?

Answer: Persons should remain in society carrying out their usual profession and, while contributing to society, internally carry on analysis and practice. In daily life, you should go to the office, carry out your work, and return home. It would be worthwhile to sacrifice some late evening entertainment, go to sleep early, and get up early the next morning to perform analytical meditation. Then have a good breakfast and go slowly to your place of work. Occasionally, when you have enough money, go to a Buddhist country for a few weeks. I think this may be practical and effective.

Question: How can we understand emptiness very simply without getting into too much intellectualized philosophy?

Answer: Is not what I have been talking about for the past few days rather simple? The main idea is that when objects are sought under analysis, they are not found, but this does not mean that they do not exist—it simply means that they lack inherent existence. If you contemplate this again and again, in time realization will definitely emerge.

Question: How do altruism and realization of emptiness unite in practice?

Answer: In the Sūtra Great Vehicle, the practices of the altruistic intention to become enlightened are the means for accumulating the collection of merit; it is under the influence of these practices that one meditates on emptiness. Similarly, meditation on emptiness accumulates wisdom. Then, influenced by ascertainment that phenomena are empty of inherent existence, one cultivates the altruistic intention to become enlightened. I will discuss how these are combined in tantra when I continue my talk.

Question: How should we help someone who is dying? What should we say to the dying person?

Answer: It is most important not to cause disturbance in the mind of a dying person, and also it is important to activate memory of a virtuous religious practice with which the person is familiar. Those who do not accept the practice of any religion should be helped to die with a peaceful, relaxed attitude. The reason for this is that, as was explained earlier in relation to the twelve links of dependent-arising, the type of attitude that one has near the time of death is extremely important with regard to what karma is activated and thus how one will be reborn in the next lifetime.

For those who are engaged in Buddhist practice, there are many different levels of reflection that a dying person can put to use—reflecting on the meaning of emptiness, cultivating an altruistic intention to become enlightened, cultivating deity yoga, engaging in practice of the winds, and even reflecting on the exalted wisdom of undifferentiable bliss and emptiness, performing the transference of consciousness, and so forth. No matter how great the benefit or power of meditation may be in the abstract, it is crucial that the dying person be drawn to a practice that is appropriate due to previous familiarity. Since near the time of death the power of alertness and so forth deteriorate, there is no sense at all in trying to force a dying person to engage in an unfamiliar practice. It is most beneficial to remind the person of a practice that is appropriate to his or her own level.

Compassion and Wisdom Combined

MANTRA

AS MENTIONED EARLIER, an altruistically motivated person matures his or her own continuum by practicing the six perfections, and matures the continuums of others by practicing the four ways of gathering students. Among the six perfections, each of the latter ones is more difficult to achieve and is more important than the former ones. The last two perfections are concentration and wisdom.

In terms of the Sūtra Vehicle, Maitreya's *Ornament for Clear Realization* presents thirty-seven paths in harmony with enlightenment for the sake of achieving liberation, and many variations of paths for the sake of achieving buddhahood. The root for all of these is the meditative stabilization described as a union of a calm abiding of the mind and special insight.

As a means of achieving this meditative stabilization quickly and powerfully, there is the Mantra (or Tantra) Vehicle, comprising four tantra sets—action, performance, yoga, and highest yoga; the three lower tantras share roughly the same general mode of procedure, although each has distinctive practices. In both the Perfection Vehicle and the Secret Mantra Vehicle practice is rooted in the altruistic intention to become enlightened and the view of the emptiness of inherent existence. The greatness of secret mantra, on the other hand, comes by way of meditative stabilization. Thus it is even said that the scriptures of secret mantra are included in the sets of discourses,[36] since meditative stabilization is their main topic.

In what way does the Secret Mantra Vehicle achieve its distinctiveness through meditative stabilization? How does it have a more profound way of enhancing the meditative stabilization that is a union of calm abiding and special insight? Motivated by the altruistic intention to become enlightened, one aims at full enlightenment; that state of buddhahood is endowed with a truth body, the fulfillment of one's own welfare, and form bodies, the fulfillment of others' welfare. These two practitioners specifically aim to achieve form bodies in order to assist others. Certain form bodies possess the major and minor marks of a buddha's body. In the Perfection Vehicle within the sūtra system, one seeks to achieve this type of body by accumulating meritorious power through practicing the six perfections under the influence of great compassion and the altruistic intention to become enlightened. In addition to these practices, the distinctive feature of tantra is to engage in a technique similar in aspect to the type of form body that is being sought—one meditates on oneself as presently having the physical body of a buddha. This practice is called deity yoga. Since this practice concords in aspect with the result one is trying to achieve, deity yoga is particularly effective and powerful.

In this way a distinctive feature of secret mantra is a yoga in which method and wisdom are indivisible. In the Perfection Vehicle, altruistic method and wisdom are separate entities that influence each other; altruistic method is affected by the force of wisdom, and wisdom is affected by the force of altruistic method. How are the two indivisible within tantra? In the practice of deity yoga, a single consciousness contains these two factors: the imagination of a divine body and the simultaneous ascertainment of its emptiness of inherent existence. The imagination of a divine body, which is in the class of compassionately vast appearances, accumulates the collection of merit; hence a mind of deity yoga fulfills the feature of altruistic method. Since the very same mind ascertains the emptiness of inherent existence of the divine body and so forth, the collection of wisdom is accumulated; thus the same mind of deity yoga fulfills the qualities of wisdom. Although method and wisdom are still separable conceptually, they are contained in the entity of one consciousness.

A yogi intentionally imagines in his or her mental consciousness the appearance of him- or herself in a divine body. When yogis imagine themselves as being a deity and realize the emptiness of that divine body, there is a difference in the impact of this realization due to this special object—the divine body—which is the substratum of emptiness.

Also, when, in the Perfection Vehicle, one meditates on the emptiness of the self and the phenomena included in the five aggregates, one does not engage in techniques to cause the substratum to keep appearing and not to disappear. In the tantra system, one specifically trains in maintaining the appearance of the divine body in the midst of ascertaining its emptiness of inherent existence. While imagining a divine body, the emptiness of inherent existence of that body is ascertained by the mode of apprehension of the same consciousness; thus it is said that a factor of the wisdom-consciousness that realizes emptiness appears as a deity.

HIGHEST YOGA TANTRA

Highest yoga tantra describes an even more profound way in which altruistic method and wisdom are undifferentiable. This is understood by focusing on more subtle physical and mental factors—the very subtle wind, or energy, and the very subtle mind, which themselves are an undifferentiable entity. To practice this level, it is necessary to forcefully stop the coarser levels of wind and mind. Highest yoga tantra describes many different techniques for doing this by placing emphasis on different places in the body. This is the practice of the channels, the winds, or internal energies, and the drops of essential fluid.

In general, the cultivation of special insight involves analytical meditation, but due to these special factors, in highest yoga tantra it is stabilizing meditation that is emphasized when cultivating special insight. Coarser levels of consciousness induce ascertainment through analysis and investigation. On the other hand, when one purposely manifests subtler levels of consciousness induced through the power of yoga (rather than at times when these happen naturally due to the power of karma, such as while dying) these subtle consciousnesses in which the coarser levels have ceased are fully capable of ascertaining meanings. If one engages in analysis at that time, it causes the subtler level to cease and a coarser level to return. Since the subtler level of I compensates for analysis—the purpose of which is to endow the mind with the capability of profound ascertainment—one does not conduct analysis at that time, and stabilizing meditation is prescribed.

Highest yoga tantra prescribes two main meditational systems for achieving a buddha body: through focusing on both very subtle wind and mind, and through focusing only on very subtle mind. In most of the highest yoga tantras of the New Translation Schools,[37] such as *Guhyasamāja* and *Chakrasamvara,* the emphasis is placed on both very subtle wind and mind in order to achieve a buddha body. In the Kālachakra system,[38] however, very subtle mind alone is emphasized, and in the practice of the great seal[39] and the great completeness[40] also the emphasis is mainly on very subtle mind.

From another perspective it is said that, among highest yoga tantras, one group focuses on the channels, winds, and drops of essential fluids in order to manifest the fundamental innate mind of clear light, and another group manifests that mind through sustaining only a nonconceptual state without focusing on channels, winds, and drops. Within the first, there are tantras that put particular emphasis on the wind yoga, as is the case with *Guhyasamāja,* and tantras that put particular emphasis on the four joys, as is the case with *Chakrasamvara.* The great seal and the great completeness are among those systems that manifest the fundamental innate mind of clear light through sustaining only a nonconceptual state.

Before engaging in the practice of tantra it is necessary for one to receive initiation, and after receiving initiation it is important to keep the pledges and the vows that have been bestowed. In initiation, one person transmits a lineage of blessing to another, and even though blessings can be gained via other methods, such as reading books, it is better to receive a blessing from a living person's mental continuum because its benefit forms more easily in the mind. Due to this, in secret tantra lamas are valued highly. We have already talked about the care one has to take with respect to accepting someone as a lama; here I will just add that it is said that when practitioners do not bear the proper form of the practice, it is an omen of the degeneration of the religion.

TANTRIC DEITIES

Although Buddhism does not have a creator god, in its many forms of initiation and so forth there are a great many gods. What are they? As discussed earlier, from the beginning of bodhisattva practice one wishes and aims to achieve the altruistically active form bodies of a buddha in order to bring vast, effective help to other sentient beings. In buddhahood, form bodies appear spontaneously and without exertion in order to assist others. Just as when there is a reflection of the moon, there has to be something to reflect it, so the spontaneous appearance of the form bodies of a buddha require beings before whom to appear. Also, whether a reflection appears clearly or unclearly, big or small, and so forth depends upon the surface on which it is reflected; similarly, the colors, shapes, and aspects of form bodies appear spontaneously and without exertion to trainees relative to their interests, dispositions, beliefs, needs, and so forth. In this way, the gods of the three lower tantras appear in aspects making use of the five pleasurable attributes of the desire realm—pleasurable visible forms, sounds, odors, tastes, and tangible objects—but without partaking of the pleasurable attributes of the joining of male and female organs. For trainees who cannot make use of these pleasurable attributes of the desire realm in the path, the form body of a buddha appears as a supreme emanation body in the aspect of a monk, as did Shākyamuni Buddha.

If trainees have the disposition and capacity to practice highest yoga tantra and if their capacities are activated, form bodies manifest to them in the aspect of male and female deities in union. Form bodies appear in a wrathful aspect to those capable of using the factor of hatred in the path, and in a peaceful aspect to those who are capable mainly of using desire. Thus form bodies appear in various ways relative to trainees' capacities.

A particular buddha could appear as a single deity but could also manifest many emanations simultaneously. For instance, Guhya-samāja manifests as thirty-two persons in a mandala, but this does not mean that there are thirty-two persons; there is only one actual person—the others are just emanations. Hence, among the hosts of deities there are many that are just emanations, or reflections, of one being.

THE VIEW IN THE FOUR ORDERS OF TIBETAN BUDDHISM

When the term "view"[41] is used, it is important to determine its meaning in context, since just as the word "feeling" can refer both to that which feels and to that which is felt, so "view" can refer either to the consciousness that views or to the object that is viewed. In highest yoga tantra, the term "view" is predominantly used to refer to that which views, the consciousness that views. According to its distinctive presentation, while there is no difference in the emptiness that is viewed, there is a difference in the subject, the great bliss consciousness that views emptiness. Referring to emptiness as the object that is viewed, Sa-ġya Paṇḍita (1182–1251) says that sūtra and mantra have the same view, and many Ge-luk-ba texts similarly speak about sūtra and mantra as having the same view.

Nevertheless, in Śa-ḡya-ba four different views are posited with respect to the four initiations in highest yoga tantra—the view of the vase initiation, the view of the secret initiation, the view of the knowledge-wisdom initiation, and the view of the word initiation. Similarly, Ge-luk-ba texts such as Jam-ȳang-shay-ba's[42] *Great Exposition of Tenets*[43] speak of highest yoga tantra as being superior due to its view, referring to the subject that views—the wisdom of great bliss. Hence, when such scholars say that there is no difference in view between sūtra and mantra, they are speaking of the object being viewed, emptiness, since sūtra and mantra do not differ with regard to it. However, when they say that sūtra and mantra differ in view, they are speaking of the consciousness that views emptiness, since highest yoga tantra presents subtler levels of mind that realize emptiness in a more powerful way. Ga-gyu-ba and Ñying-ma-ba texts similarly say that the view of mantra is superior to that of sūtra; all of them refer to a distinctive, subtler type of mind.

Śa-ḡya-ba texts present a view of the undifferentiability of cyclic existence and nirvana, saying that it is to be delineated in terms of the causal continuum that is the basis-of-all. There are slightly different explanations of this causal continuum among the Indian *paṇḍitas* and within Śa-ḡya-ba, but it generally refers to the real nature of the mind. From a different perspective, the *Guhyasamāja Tantra* speaks of students of different levels of capacity; the supremely capable student is called the "jewel-like person," who could be described as the causal continuum that is the basis-of-all.

In Śa-ḡya-ba, the causal continuum is identified by the great scholar Mang-tö-lu-drup-gya-tso[44] as the fundamental innate mind of clear light. In another interpretation within Śa-ḡya-ba it is identified as all of the impure aggregates, constituents, and sense spheres of a person. It is also said that, in the causal continuum, all of the phenomena of cyclic existence are complete in terms of nature, all of the phenomena of the path are complete in terms of qualities, and all of the phenomena of buddhahood are complete in terms of effects.

With respect to the equality of cyclic existence and nirvana, in the sūtra system Nāgārjuna says in his *Sixty Stanzas of Reasoning:*

> Both cyclic existence and nirvana
> Do not [inherently] exist.
> Just that which is knowledge of cyclic existence
> Is called "nirvana."[45]

In the sūtra system the reality—into which all true sufferings and sources of suffering are extinguished when one has thoroughly understood the meaning of the absence of inherent existence of cyclic existence—is nirvana. A Śa-ǧya-ba presentation of the equality of cyclic existence and nirvana explains that the impure phenomena of the mental and physical aggregates and so forth primordially exist as pure mental and physical aggregates. Four "mandalas" are presented as the foundation—these being the channels of the body, the winds, the drops of essential fluid, and letters. These are viewed as entities of the four bodies of a buddha.

According to Mang-tö-lu-drup-gya-tso, all of the phenomena of cyclic existence and nirvana are to be viewed as the sport, or reflection, of the fundamental innate mind of clear light, since they all share the same taste in the sphere of clear light. This is the view of the undifferentiability of cyclic existence and nirvana. Thus, the doctrine of the undifferentiability of cyclic existence and nirvana stems from the fundamental mind.

In Ga-gyu-ba, meditation on the great seal is done by way of four yogas—one-pointed, nonelaborative, one-taste, and nonmeditative. The first two are said to be in common with the sūtra path; through one-pointed yoga, calm abiding of the mind is achieved, and through non-elaborative yoga, special insight into emptiness is achieved. Through one-taste yoga, an extraordinary special insight is achieved in which all appearing and occurring phenomena are seen as one taste in the sphere of the fundamental innate mind of clear light. When this path, which is unique to tantra, increases in strength, it becomes non-meditative yoga. As Nāgārjuna says in his *Five Stages*,[46] which is concerned with the system of the *Guhyasamāja Tantra*, when one arrives at the level of the union of pure body and pure mind, there is nothing new to learn.

About the view of the great seal it is said:

> The very mind is the innate truth body.
> Appearances are the waves of the innate truth body.

The very mind, or basic mind, is the innate truth body—the fundamental mind of clear light. All pure and impure appearances are the sport of that truth body; they dawn from within the sphere of the fundamental mind of clear light.

In Ge-luk-ba, it would not be fitting to claim that a view like that of the great seal is the same as the view of the Middle Way, but it could be said to be a *special* view of the Middle Way. Within Ge-luk-ba such a special view is found in meditations on the view of the Middle Way that are combined with highest yoga tantra. When one thinks in these terms, the union of bliss and emptiness in Ge-luk-ba presentations of highest yoga tantra and particularly the innate level of the union of bliss and emptiness are the same as that of the great seal. Ge-luk-ba texts on sūtra and even on mantra emphasize the view as the object viewed, that is to say, emptiness; nevertheless, their texts on mantra speak frequently about the view in terms of the subject, the viewing consciousness. Also, it is said that all pure and impure phenomena, understood as the sport of emptiness, are also to be seen as the sport of the subject, the viewing consciousness, the innate mind of clear light. As Nāgārjuna says in his *Five Stages:*

> The yogi, while abiding in the illusion-like meditative
> stabilization,
> [Is to view] everything like that.

The yogi, while abiding in illusion-like meditative stabilization, is to view all appearing and occurring phenomena—environments and beings within them—as the sport of illusion-like meditative stabilization.

In the view of the great completeness, the mode of explanation is very different, but the referent is exactly the same. As a source for this I mainly rely on the great scholar and remarkable yogi Do-drup-chen Jik-may-den-bay-nyi-ma.[47] In the great completeness the root reference is to the fundamental innate mind of clear light, but it is called "ordinary consciousness."[48] A distinction is drawn between mind[49] and basic mind;[50] "ordinary consciousness" refers to basic mind.

In the Ñying-ma-ba system, highest yoga tantra itself is divided into three categories—*mahāyoga, anuyoga,* and *atiyoga.* Atiyoga, or the great completeness, is also divided into three—the class of mind,[51] the class of the great vastness,[52] and the class of quintessential instructions.[53] As Do-drup-chen Jik-may-den bay-nyi-ma says, all of the texts of highest yoga tantra in all of the New Translation and Old Translation Schools teach only the practice of the fundamental innate mind of clear light. The difference between them is explained as follows: Within other systems, in the beginning stages of practice one makes use of many practices that involve conceptuality, through which the fundamental innate mind of clear light is manifested. In the great completeness, on the other hand, from the beginning the utilization of conceptuality is not stressed; emphasis is placed on basic mind in dependence upon quintessential instructions. This is why it is called a doctrine free from exertion.

Because in the great completeness tremendous emphasis is placed on the fundamental innate mind of clear light, it includes an uncommon presentation of the two truths, called the special two truths.[54] It could roughly be said that what is fundamental and innate is the ultimate truth and, relative to that, anything that is adventitious is a conventional truth. From this perspective, the fundamental innate mind of clear light is empty of all conventional truths that are adventitious phenomena, and thus it is an "other-emptiness"; that is to say, it is empty of what is other. Still, the fundamental innate mind of clear light is said to have a nature of essential purity and hence does not pass beyond the nature of the emptiness of inherent existence set forth in the middle wheel of Buddha's teaching.

This other-emptiness is set forth in a context of compatibility between the emptiness of inherent existence of the middle wheel and the buddha nature as it is presented in the third wheel. Because of this, it is described in some oral traditions as a "good" other-emptiness, whereas "bad" other-emptiness is a teaching that stresses only the buddha nature at the expense of the middle wheel, consequently advocating that the buddha nature does inherently exist. In this way, many qualified scholars from all of the schools of Tibetan Buddhism—Nying-ma-ba, Sa-gya-ba, Ga-gyu-ba, and Ge-luk-ba— have specifically refuted an other-emptiness that both presents a final truth that is itself inherently existent and looks down on the emptiness of inherent existence as an annihilatory self-emptiness to be derided.

As is said in an oral transmission from the great lama Kyen-dzay Jam-yang-chö-gyi-lo-drö,[55] when the great Nying-ma-ba adept Long-chen-rap-jam[56] gives a presentation of the ground, path, and fruit, he does so mainly from the perspective of the enlightened state of a buddha, whereas the Sa-gya-ba presentation is mainly from the perspective of the spiritual experience of a yogi on the path, and the Ge-luk-ba presentation is mainly from the perspective of how phenomena appear to ordinary sentient beings. This statement appears to be worthy of considerable reflection; through it, many misunderstandings can be removed.[57]

Achieving a State of Supreme Altruistic Effectiveness

In practicing systems that emphasize both wind and mind, one achieves a union of pure body and pure mind—illusory body and mind of clear light—in dependence upon which the supremely altruistically effective state of buddhahood is attained. In the uncommon mode of procedure of the mother tantras, buddhahood is achieved by way of a rainbow body. In the Kālachakra system, which emphasizes mainly the mind, buddhahood is attained in dependence upon a union of a body of empty form and supreme immutable bliss. The Ñying-ma-ba system of the great completeness also emphasizes mainly the mind. Therein, all of the coarse factors of one's body are consumed in dependence upon the completion of four levels of appearance and, much as in the system of the mother tantras, one achieves a rainbow body of great transference. All of these embodiments of wisdom and compassion exist for the sake of helping other beings extricate themselves from the round of suffering impelled by ignorance.

Notes

INTRODUCTION

1 The dating follows Southern Buddhist traditions.

2 Because demigods are also gods, their realm is often combined with that of the gods, resulting in a drawing with five, not six, sectors.

3 In the first of his three books entitled *Stages of Meditation;* see Ācārya rGyal mtshan rnam grol, *slob dpon kamalashīlas mdzad pa'i bsgom rim thog mtha' bar gsum* (Varanasi, India: dbus bod kyi ches mtho'i gtsug lag slob gnyer khang, 1985), 5.6ff.

4 *ma rig pa, avidyā.*

5 *'du byed kyi las, saṃskārakarma.*

6 *rnam shes, vijñāna.*

7 *ming gzugs, nāmarūpa.*

8 *skye mched, āyatana.*

9 *reg pa, sparśa.*

10 *tshor ba, vedanā.*

11 *sred pa, tṛṣṇā.*

12 *len pa, upādāna.*

13 *srid pa, bhava.*

14 *skye ba, jāti.*

15 *rga shi, jarāmaraṇa.*

16 Adapted from stanza 24 of Chandrakīrti's *Supplement to (Nāgārjuna's) "Treatise on the Middle"* (*dbu ma la 'jug pa, madhyamakāvatāra;* Peking 5261, Peking 5262, vol. 98).

17 *abhyudaya, mngon mtho.* For a discussion of high status, see Jeffrey Hopkins. *Buddhist Advice for Living and Liberation: Nāgārjuna's Precious Garland* (Ithaca: Snow Lion, 1998), 31–45.

18 *tsong kha pa blo bzang grags pa;* 1357–1419. See ibid.

19 *nus pa.*

20 In order to purify this process, certain initiations in highest yoga tantra follow this pattern in pure form; see Dalai Lama, Tenzin Gyatso and Jeffrey Hopkins, *The Kālachakra Tantra: Rite of Initiation for the Stage of Generation* (London: Wisdom Publications, 1985; second revd. edition, Boston, 1989), 93–97, 264–266, and so forth.

21 *'phangs 'bras.*

22 Adapted from Jeffrey Hopkins, *Meditation on Emptiness* (London: Wisdom, 1983; rev. ed., Boston: Wisdom Publications, 1996), 279; for other versions, see *Meditation on Emptiness,* 707–11.

23 *de ma bdag rkyen, samanantarapratyāya.*

24 *bdag rkyen, adhipatipratyāya.* Other translations include "proprietary condition" and "empowering condition."

25 *dmigs rkyen, ālambanapratyaya.*

26 *nyer len, upādāna.*

27 Stanza 35. See Jeffrey Hopkins, *Buddhist Advice for Living and Liberation: Nāgārjuna's Precious Garland* (Ithaca: Snow Lion, 1998), p. 98.

28 Ibid., stanza 36.

LECTURES

1 *sā lu'i ljang pa'i mdo, śālistambasūtra*; P876, vol. 34.

2 *rang bzhin, prakṛti; spyi gtso bo, sāmānyapradhāna.*

3 Sāṃkhya is a non-Buddhist Indian system that presents two categories of existents: pure consciousness, called the person, and material phenomena, the most basic of which is the general principal, also called the fundamental nature. Although the latter is permanent, it is said that from it all material phenomena arise.

4 For a series of lectures structured around the four noble truths, see Dalai Lama XIV, *The Dalai Lama at Harvard: Lectures on the Buddhist Path to Peace* (Ithaca: Snow Lion Publications, 1989).

5 *kun 'byung, samudaya.*

6 *srid pa'i 'khor lo cha lnga pa.* The one pictured here has six sectors, with separate sectors for gods and demigods.

7 For more about this story, see Sermey Geshe Lobsang Tharchin, *King Udrayana and the Wheel of Life* (Howell, NJ: Mahayana Sutra and Tantra Press, 1984), pp. 7–19.

8 *stong pa nyid bdun cu pa'i tshig le'ur byas pa, śūnyatāsaptatikārikā;* P5227, vol.95; Toh 3827, Tokyo *sde dge* vol.1. See the bibliography for editions and translations.

9 *'jig tshogs la lta ba, satkāyadṛṣṭi.*

10 See *Meditation on Emptiness* for the five types of reasoning.

11 If well-constructed, a potter's wheel will keep turning for a long period of time.

12 *bsam pa'i las.*

13 *sems pa'i las.*

14   In lectures at Harvard, the Dalai Lama gave the following examples:

> An example of the first would be to deliberately kill a mosquito.
> Then, let us suppose that an insect was bothering you, and you
> wanted very much to kill it, but someone distracts you. In this case,
> you have karmically accumulated the motivation but you did not
> carry out the action; this is an action deliberated but not done. An
> example of an action done but without deliberation would be to kill
> a mosquito by just moving one's hand without having intended to
> do so; you killed it, but not deliberately. The fourth type is when
> one neither has the motivation nor carries out the action.
> *The Dalai Lama at Harvard,* p. 60.

15   An action infuses, or deposits, a predisposing potency in the mind when it
is about to cease. Both the action and the predisposition that it deposits in
the mind are called *karma.*

16   *kun gzhi rnam par shes pa, ālayavijñāna.*

17   For a discussion of levels of mind in connection with the process of dying,
see Lati Rinbochay and Jeffrey Hopkins, *Death, Intermediate State, and
Rebirth in Tibetan Buddhism* (London: Rider, 1979; rpt. Ithaca: Snow Lion
Publications, 1980).

18   *ming gzhi.*

19   Feeling and discrimination are two from a standard list of fifty-one mental
factors. See *The Dalai Lama at Harvard,* pp. 75–76.

20   *chos mngon pa'i mdzod, abhidharmakośa;* chapter three. See the Bibliography
for editions and translations.

21   *dmigs rkyen, ālambanapratyaya.*

22   *bdag rkyen, adhipatipratyaya.*

23   *de ma bdag rkyen, samanantarapratyāya.*

24   *zhol ba.*

25 *zhugs pa.*

26 *rten, pratītya.*

27 For more discussion of many of the points raised here, see *MindScience: An East-West Dialogue* (Boston: Wisdom Publications, 1991).

28 For many ways of countering depression, see the index of *The Dalai Lama at Harvard.*

29 *dgra bcom pa, arhan.* With respect to the translation of *arhan/arhant (dgra bcom pa)* as "foe destroyer," I do this to accord with the usual Tibetan translation of the term and to assist in capturing the flavor of oral and written traditions that frequently refer to this etymology. Arhans have overcome the foe, which is the afflictive emotions *(nyon mongs, kleśa),* the chief of which is ignorance, the conception (according to the Consequence School) that persons and phenomena are established by way of their own character.

The Indian and Tibetan translators were also aware of the etymology of *arhan* as "worthy one," as they translated the name of the "founder" of the Jaina system, Arhat, as *mchod 'od* "worthy of worship" (see Jam-ȳang-shay-ba's *Great Exposition of Tenets, ka* 62a.3). Also, they were aware of Chandrakīrti's gloss of the term as "worthy one" in his *Clear Words:* "Because of being worthy of worship by the world of gods, humans, and demigods, they are called *arhans*" *(sadevamānuṣāsurāl lokāt pūnārhatvād arhannityuchyate* [Poussin, 486.5], *lha dang mi dang lha ma yin du bcas pa'i 'jig rten gyis mchod par 'os pas dgra bcom pa zhes brjod la* [409.20, Tibetan Cultural Printing Press edition; also, P5260, vol. 98 75.2.2)]. Also, they were aware of Haribhadra's twofold etymology in his *Illumination of the Eight Thousand Stanza Perfection of Wisdom Sūtra.* In the context of the list of epithets qualifying the retinue of the Buddha at the beginning of the sūtra (see Unrai Wogihara, ed., *Abhisamayālaṃkārālokā Prajñā-pāramitā-vyākhyā, The Work of Haribhadra* [Tokyo: The Toyo Bunko, 1932–35; reprint ed., Tokyo: Sankibo Buddhist Book Store], 1973, 8.18), Haribhadra says:

They are called *arhant* [=worthy one, from root *arh* "to be worthy"] since they are worthy of worship, religious donations, and being assembled together in a group, etc. (W9.8–9: *sarva evātra pūjā-dakṣiṇā-gaṇa-parikarṣādy-ārhatay-arhantaḥ;* P5189, 67.5.7: *'dir thams*

*cad kyang mchod pa dang // yon dang tshogs su 'dub la sogs par 'os pas
na dgra bcom pa'o).*

Also:

> They are called *arhant* [=foe destroyer, *arihan*] because they have
> destroyed *(hata)* the foe *(ari).*
> (W 10.18: *hatāritvād arhantaḥ;* P5189, 69.3.6. *dgra rnams bcom pas
> na dgra bcom pa'o).*

(My thanks to Gareth Sparham for the references to Haribhadra.) Thus,
we are not dealing with an ignorant misconception of a term, but a considered preference in the face of alternative etymologies—"foe destroyer"
requiring a not unusual *i* infix to make *arihan, ari* meaning enemy and *han*
meaning to kill, and thus "foe destroyer." Unfortunately, one word in English cannot convey both this meaning and "worthy of worship"; thus, I have
gone with what clearly has become the predominant meaning in Tibet.
(For an excellent discussion of the two etymologies of *arhat* in Buddhism
and Jainism, see L.M. Joshi's "Facets of Jaina Religiousness in Comparative
Light," L.D. Series 85, [Ahmedabad: L.D. Institute of Indology, May 1981],
pp. 53–58.)

30   For more discussion of these seven types of awareness, see Lati Rinbochay
and Elizabeth Napper, *Mind in Tibetan Buddhism* (London: Rider and
Company, 1980; Ithaca: Snow Lion Publications, 1980).

31   *Fundamental Treatise on the Middle, Called "Wisdom,"* XVIII.5 *(dbu ma'i
bstan bcos/ dbu ma rtsa ba'i tshig le'ur byas pa shes rab ces bya ba, madhya-
makaśāstra/ prajñānāmamūlamadhyamakakārikā),* P5224, vol. 95. See the
bibliography for editions and translations.

32   *stong pa nyid kyis.*

33   *stong pa nyid du.*

34   *pad ma dkar po,* 1527–92.

35   *byang chub sems dpa'i spyod pa la 'jug pa, bodhicāryāvatāra.* See the bibliography for editions and translations.

36   *mdo sde, sūtrānta.*

37 Śa-ḡya, Ḡa-gyu, and Ge-luk.

38 For discussion of the Kālachakra system by the Dalai Lama, see Tenzin Gyatso and Jeffrey Hopkins, *The Kālachakra Tantra: Rite of Initiation for the Stage of Generation* (London: Wisdom Publications, 1985; second rev. edition, Boston: Wisdom Publications, 1999).

39 *mahāmudrā, phyag rgya chen po.*

40 *rdzogs chen.*

41 *lta ba.*

42 *'jam dbyangs bzhad pa'i rdo rje ngag dbang brtson grus*; 1648–1721.

43 *grub mtha'i rnam bshad rang gzhan grub mtha' kun dang zab don mchog tu gsal ba kun bzang zhing gi nyi ma lung rigs rgya mtsho skye dgu'i re ba kun skong/ grub mtha' chen mo.* See the bibliography for editions and translations.

44 *mang thos klu sgrub rgya mtsho*; 1523–96.

45 *rigs pa drug cu pa'i tshig le'ur byas pa, yuktiṣaṣṭikākarikā*; stanza 7. For the edited Tibetan with Sanskrit fragments and English translation, see Chr. Lindtner in *Nagarjuniana,* Indiske Studier 4 (Copenhagen: Akademisk Forlag, 1982), pp. 100–119.

46 *rim pa lnga pa, pañcakrama*; P2667, vol. 61.

47 *rdo grub chen 'jigs med bstan pa'i nyi ma*; 1865–1926.

48 *tha mal pa'i shes pa.*

49 *sems.*

50 *rig pa.*

51 *sems sde.*

52 *klong sde.*

53 *man ngag gi sde.*

54 *lhag pa'i bden gnyis.*

55 *mkhyen brtse 'jam dbyangs chos kyi blo gros,* died 1959.

56 *klong chen rab 'byams,* 1308–63.

57 For more on how the four orders of Tibetan Buddhism come down to the same thought, see the final chapter in The Fourteenth Dalai Lama, His Holiness Tenzin Gyatso, *Kindness, Clarity, and Insight* (Ithaca: Snow Lion Publications, 1984).

Glossary

ENGLISH	SANSKRIT	TIBETAN
action	karma	las
affirming negative	paryudāsapratiṣedha	ma yin dgag
afflictive emotion/affliction	kleśa	nyon mongs
afflictive obstruction	kleśāvaraṇa	nyon sgrib/ nyon mongs pa'i sgrib pa
aggregate	skandha	phung po
aging and death	jarāmaraṇa	rga shi
attachment	tṛṣṇā	sred pa
birth	jāti	skye ba
bodhisattva	bodhisattva	byang chub sems dpa'
compositional action	saṃskārakarma	'du byed kyi las
compounded phenomenon	saṃskṛta	'dus byas
conceptuality/conceptual consciousness	vikalpa	rtog pa
consciousness	vijñāna	rnam shes
contact	sparśa	reg pa

conventional truth	saṃvṛtisatya	kun rdzob bden pa
conventionally	vyavahāratas	tha snyad du
correctly assuming consciousness	manaḥparīkṣā	yid dpyod
cyclic existence	saṃsāra	'khor ba
desire realm	kāmadhātu	'dod khams
discipline	vinaya	'dul ba
doctrine	dharma	chos
doubt	vicikitsā/ saṃśaya	the tshom
emptiness	śūnyatā	stong pa nyid
entity	vastu	ngo bo
entity/substantial entity	dravya	rdzas
exist validly	pramāṇasiddha	tshad mas grub pa
existence	bhava	srid pa
existent	sat	yod pa
existing by way of its own character	svalakṣaṇasiddha	rang gi mtshan nyid kyis grub pa
existing in its own right/ existing from its own side	svarūpasiddha	rang ngos nas grub pa
existing inherently	svabhāvasiddha	rang bzhin gyis grub pa

external object	bāhyārtha	phyi don
feeling	vedanā	tshor ba
foe destroyer	arhan	dgra bcom pa
form	rūpa	gzugs
form body	rūpakāya	gzugs sku
form realm	rūpadhātu	gzugs khams
formless realm khams	ārūpyadhātu	gzugs med
fruit	phala	'bras bu
grasping	upādāna	len pa
hearer	śrāvaka	nyan thos
highest enlightenment	anuttarasambuddha	bla na med pa'i byang chub
ignorance	avidyā	ma rig pa
impermanent	anitya	mi rtag pa
imputedly existent	prajñaptisat	btags yod
inferential valid cognition	anumānapramāṇa	rjes su dpag pa'i tshad ma
inherently existent	svabhāvasiddha	rang bzhin gyis grub pa
jewel/superior rarity	ratna	dkon mchog
latency/predisposition	vāsanā	bag chags
manifest knowledge	abhidharma	chos mngon pa

meditative stabilization	samādhi	ting nge 'dzin
mental and physical aggregates	skandha	phung po
mental consciousness	manovijñāna	yid kyi rnam shes
mental factor	caitta	sems byung
mind	citta	sems
mind generation of altruistic aspiration to highest enlightenment	bodhicittaparamotpāda	byang chub mchog tu sems bskyed pa
mind-basis-of-all	ālayavijñāna	kun gzhi rnam par shes pa
mistaken consciousness	bhrāntijñāna	'khrul shes
name and form	nāmarūpa	ming gzugs
negative phenomenon	pratiṣedha	dgag pa
non-affirming negative	prasajyapratiṣedha	med dgag
object	viṣaya	yul
object of knowledge	jñeya	shes bya
obstruction to liberation/ afflictive obstruction	kleśāvaraṇa	nyon sgrib
obstruction to omniscience of all phenomena	jñeyāvaraṇa	shes sgrib
path	mārga	lam
path of accumulation	saṃbhāramārga	tshogs lam
path of meditation	bhāvanāmārga	sgom lam

path of no more learning	aśaikṣamārga	mi slob lam
path of preparation	prayogamārga	sbyor lam
path of seeing	darśanamārga	mthong lam
person	puruṣa	skyes bu
person's emptiness of being permanent, unitary, and independent	nityaikasvatantra -śūnyapudgala	gang zag rtag gcig rang dbang can gyis stong pa
product	kṛta	byas pa
reason	hetu	gtan tshigs
self	ātman	bdag
selflessness of persons	pudgalanairātmya	gang zag gi bdag med
selflessness of phenomena	dharmanairātmya	chos kyi bdag med
sentient being	sattva	sems can
sets of discourses	sūtrānta	mdo sde
six spheres	ṣaḍāyatana	skye mched drug
solitary realizer	pratyekabuddha	rang sangs rgyas
space	ākāśa	nam mkha'
special insight	vipaśyanā	lhag mthong
spiritual community	saṅgha	dge 'dun

substantially established	dravyasiddha	rdzas grub
substantially existent	dravyasat	rdzas yod
sūtra	sūtra	mdo
tangible object	spraṣṭavya	reg bya
thing/functioning thing	bhāva	dngos po
truly established/truly existent	satyasiddha	bden par grub pa
truly existent/truly established	satyasat	bden par yod pa
truth	satya	bden pa
truth body	dharmakāya	chos sku
ultimate truth	paramārthasatya	don dam bden pa
ultimately	paramārthatas	don dam par
uncompounded [phenomenon]	asaṃskṛta	'dus ma byas
valid cognition	pramāṇa	tshad ma
wrong consciousness	viparyayajña	log shes

Bibliography

Indian and Tibetan treatises are listed alphabetically by author in the second section. Other works are listed alphabetically by author in the third section. 'P,' standing for 'Peking edition,' refers to the *Tibetan Tripiṭaka* (Tokyo-Kyoto: Tibetan Tripiṭaka Research Foundation, 1956).

SŪTRA

Rice Seedling Sūtra
śālistambasūtra
sā lu'i ljang pa'i mdo
P876, vol. 34
Sanskrit and Tibetan texts: *Śālistamba Sūtra, Pratitya-Samutpāda-vibhaṅga Nirdeśasūtra*, and *Pratītyasamutpādagāthā Sūtra*. N. Aiyaswami Sastri, ed. Adyar, Madras: Vasanta Press, The Theosophical Society, 1950

SANSKRIT AND TIBETAN WORKS

Chandrakīrti (*zla ba grags pa*, seventh century)

Clear Words, Commentary on (Nāgārjuna's) "Treatise on the Middle"
mūlamadhyamakavṛttiprasannapadā
dbu ma rtsa ba'i 'grel pa tshig gsal ba
P5260, vol. 98
Also: Dharamsala: Tibetan Publishing House, 1968
Sanskrit: *Mūlamadhyamakakārikās de Nāgārjuna avec la Prasannapadā commentaire de Candrakīrti*. Louis de la Vallée Poussin, ed. Bibliotheca Buddhica IV. Osnabrück: Biblio Verlag, 1970.

English translation (Ch.I, XXV): T. Stcherbatsky. *Conception of Buddhist Nirvāṇa*. Leningrad: Office of the Academy of Sciences of the USSR, 1927;

revised rpt. Delhi: Motilal Banarsidass, 1978, pp. 77–222.

English translation (Ch.II): Jeffrey Hopkins. "Analysis of Coming and Going." Dharamsala: Library of Tibetan Works and Archives, 1974.

Partial English translation: Mervyn Sprung. *Lucid Exposition of the Middle Way, the Essential Chapters from the Prasannapadā of Candrakīrti translated from the Sanskrit*. London: Routledge, 1979 and Boulder: Prajñā Press, 1979.

French translation (Ch.II–IV, VI–IX, XI, XXIII, XXIV, XXVI, XXVII): Jacques May. *Prasannapadā Madhyamaka-vṛtti, douze chapitres traduits du sanscrit et du tibétain*. Paris: Adrien-Maisonneuve, 1959.

French translation (Ch.XVIII–XXII): J.W. de Jong. *Cinq chapitres de la Prasannapadā*. Paris: Geuthner, 1949.

French translation (Ch.XVII): É. Lamotte. "Le Traité de l'acte de Vasubandhu, Karmasiddhiprakaraṇa," *Mélanges Chinois et Bouddhiques* 4 (1936): 265–88.

German translation (Ch.V and XII–XVI): St. Schayer. *Ausgewählte Kapitel aus der Prasannapadā*. Warszawa: W. Krakowie, 1931.

German translation (Ch.X): St. Schayer. "Feuer und Brennstoff." *Rocznik Orientalistyczny* 7 (1931): 26–52.

Jam-ȳang-shay-b̄a (*'jam dbyangs bzhad pa*, 1648–1721)

Great Exposition of Tenets: Explanation of 'Tenets,' Sun of the Land of Samantabhadra Brilliantly Illuminating All of Our Own and Others' Tenets and the Meaning of the Profound [Emptiness], Ocean of Scripture and Reasoning Fulfilling All Hopes of All Beings
grub mtha' chen mo/ grub mtha'i rnam bshad rang gzhan grub mtha' kun dang zab don mchog tu gsal ba kun bzang zhing gi nyi ma lung rigs rgya mtsho skye dgu'i re ba kun skong
Mussoorie: Dalama, 1962

English translation (beginning of the chapter on the Consequence School): Jeffrey Hopkins. In *Meditation on Emptiness*. London: Wisdom Publications, 1983; rev. ed., Boston: Wisdom Publications, 1996.

Nāgārjuna (*klu sgrub*, first to second century C.E.)

Treatise on the Middle/ Fundamental Treatise on the Middle, Called "Wisdom"

madhyamakaśāstra/prajñānāmamūlamadhyamakakārikā
dbu ma'i bstan bcos/ dbu ma rtsa ba'i tshig le'ur byas pa shes rab ces bya ba
P5224, vol. 95

Edited Sanskrit: *Nāgārjuna, Mūlamadhyamakakārikāh*. J.W. de Jong, ed. Adyar: Adyar Library and Research Centre, 1977. Also: Chr. Lindtner in Nāgārjuna's Filosofiske Vaerker. Indiske Studier 2, pp. 177–215. Copenhagen: Akademisk Forlag, 1982.

English translation: Frederick Streng. *Emptiness: A Study in Religious Meaning.* Nashville, New York: Abingdon Press, 1967. Also: Kenneth Inada. *Nāgārjuna: A Translation of his Mūlamadhyamakakārikā.* Tokyo, The Hokuseido Press, 1970. Also: David J. Kalupahana. *Nāgārjuna: The Philosophy of the Middle Way.* Albany: State University Press of New York, 1986. Also: Jay L. Garfield. *The Fundamental Wisdom of the Middle Way.* New York: Oxford University Press, 1995.

Italian translation: R. Gnoli. *Nāgārjuna: Madhyamaka Kārikā, Le stanze del cammino di mezzo.* Enciclopedia di autori classici 61. Turin: P. Boringhieri, 1961.

Danish translation: Chr. Lindtner in *Nāgārjuna's Filosofiske Vaerker.* Indiske Studier 2, pp. 67–135. Copenhagen: Akademisk Forlag, 1982.

Seventy Stanzas on Emptiness
śūnyatāsaptatikārikā
stong pa nyid bdun cu pa'i tshig le'ur byas pa
P5227, vol.95; Toh 3827, Tokyo *sde dge* vol.1
Edited Tibetan and English translation: Chr. Lindtner in *Nagarjuniana*. Indiske Studier 4, pp.34–69. Copenhagen: Akademisk Forlag, 1982.

English translation: David Ross Komito. *Nāgārjuna's "Seventy Stanzas": A Buddhist Psychology of Emptiness.* Ithaca: Snow Lion Publications, 1987.

Sixty Stanzas of Reasoning
yuktiṣaṣṭikākārikā
rigs pa drug cu pa'i tshig le'ur byas pa
P5227, vol. 95; Toh 3827, Tokyo *sde dge* vol. 1
Edited Tibetan with Sanskrit fragments and English translation: Chr. Lindtner in *Nagarjuniana.* Indiske Studier 4, pp. 100–119. Copenhagen: Akademisk Forlag, 1982.

Shāntideva (*zhi ba lha*, eighth century)

A Guide to a Bodhisattva's Way of Life/ Engaging in the Bodhisattva Deeds
bodhi[sattva]caryāvatāra
byang chub sems dpa'i spyod pa la 'jug pa
P5272, vol. 99
Sanskrit and Tibetan texts: Vidhushekara Bhattacharya, ed. *Bodhicaryāvatāra.*
Bibliotheca Indica, vol. 280. Calcutta: The Asiatic Society, 1960.

English translation: Stephen Batchelor. *A Guide to the Bodhisattva's Way of Life.*
Dharamsala: Library of Tibetan Works and Archives, 1979. Also: Marion Matics.
Entering the Path of Enlightenment. New York: Macmillan Co., 1970. Also: Kate
Crosby and Andrew Skilton. *The Bodhicaryāvatāra.* Oxford: Oxford University
Press, 1996. Also: Padmakara Translation Group. *The Way of the Bodhisattva.*
Boston: Shambhala, 1997. Also: Vesna A. Wallace and B. Alan Wallace. *A Guide
to the Bodhisattva Way of Life.* Ithaca: Snow Lion, 1997.

Contemporary commentary by Geshe Kelsang Gyatso. *Meaningful to Behold.*
London: Wisdom Publications, 1980

Vasubandhu (*dbyig gnyen*, fl.360)

Treasury of Knowledge
abhidharmakośakārikā
chos mngon pa'i mdzod kyi tshig le'ur byas pa
P5590, vol. 115
Sanskrit text: P. Pradhan, ed. *Abhidharmakośabhāṣyam of Vasubandhu.* Patna:
Jayaswal Research Institute, 1975

French translation: Louis de la Vallée Poussin. *L'Abhidharmakośa de Vasubandhu.*
6 vols. Bruxelles: Institut Belge des Hautes Études Chinoises, 1971.

English translation from the French: Leo M. Pruden, *Abhidharmakośabhāṣyam.*
4 vols. Freemont, CA.: Asian Humanities Press, 1988–89.

OTHER WORKS

Dalai Lama XIV, Benson, Thurman, Goleman, et al. *Mind Science: An East-West
Dialogue.* Boston: Wisdom Publications, 1991.

Gyatso, Tenzin, Dalai Lama XIV. *The Dalai Lama at Harvard: Lectures on the Buddhist Path to Peace*. Trans. and ed. Jeffrey Hopkins. Ithaca: Snow Lion Publications, 1989.

Gyatso, Tenzin, Dalai Lama XIV, and Jeffrey Hopkins. *The Kālachakra Tantra: Rite of Initiation for the Stage of Generation*. London: Wisdom Publications, 1985; rev. ed., Boston:Wisdom Publications, 1999.

Gyatso, Tenzin, Dalai Lama XIV. *Kindness, Clarity, and Insight*. Jeffrey Hopkins, trans. and ed.; Elizabeth Napper, co-editor. Ithaca: Snow Lion Publications, 1984.

Hopkins, Jeffrey. *Meditation on Emptiness*. London: Wisdom Publications, 1983.

Joshi, L.M. "Facets of Jaina Religiousness in Comparative Light," L.D. Series 85. Ahmedabad: L.D. Institute of Indology, May 1981. pp. 53–58.

Lati Rinbochay and Elizabeth Napper. *Mind in Tibetan Buddhism*. London: Rider, 1980; rpt. Ithaca: Snow Lion Publications, 1980.

Lati Rinbochay and Jeffrey Hopkins. *Death, Intermediate State, and Rebirth in Tibetan Buddhism*. London: Rider, 1979; Ithaca: Snow Lion Publications, 1980.

Lindtner, Christian. *Nagarjuniana*. Indiske Studier 4. Copenhagen: Akademisk Forlag, 1982.

Poussin, Louis de la Vallée. *L'Abhidharmakośa de Vasubandhu*. 6 vols. Bruxelles: Institut Belge des Hautes Études Chinoises, 1971.

Tharchin, Sermey Geshe Lobsang. *King Udrayana and the Wheel of Life*. Howell, NJ: Mahayana Sutra and Tantra Press, 1984.

Wogihara, Unrai, ed. *Abhisamayālaṃkārālokā Prajñā-pāramitā-vyākhyā. The Work of Haribhadra*. Tokyo: Toyo Bunko, 1932–35; rpt. ed., Tokyo: Sankibo Buddhist Book Store, 1973.

Index

*More Wisdom
from His Holiness the Dalai Lama*

BUDDHISM
One Teacher, Many Traditions
with Venerable Thubten Chodron
Foreword by Bhante Gunaratana
Preface by Venerable Thubten Chodron

THE MIDDLE WAY
Faith Grounded in Reason
Translated by Thupten Jinpa

THE WORLD OF TIBETAN BUDDHISM
An Overview of Its Philosophy and Practice
Translated, edited, and annotated by Geshe Thupten Jinpa

ESSENCE OF THE HEART SUTRA
The Dalai Lama's Heart of Wisdom Teachings
Edited by Geshe Thupten Jinpa

PRACTICING WISDOM
The Perfection of Shantideva's Bodhisattva Way

MIND IN COMFORT AND EASE
The Vision of Enlightenment in the Great Perfection
Foreword by Sogyal Rinpoche

OPENING THE EYE OF NEW AWARENESS
Translated and introduced by Donald S. Lopez, Jr.

SLEEPING, DREAMING, AND DYING
An Exploration of Consciousness with the Dalai Lama
Edited by Francisco Varela

MINDSCIENCE
An East-West Dialogue

IMAGINE ALL THE PEOPLE
*A Conversation with the Dalai Lama on Money, Politics,
and Life As It Could Be*

MEDITATION ON THE NATURE OF MIND
With Khöntön Peljor Lhundrub and José Ignacio Cabezón

THE GOOD HEART
A Buddhist Perspective on the Teachings of Jesus
Edited by Robert Kiely
Introduction by Laurence Freeman
Translated by Geshe Thupten Jinpa

THE COMPASSIONATE LIFE
Translated and introduced by Donald S. Lopez, Jr.
SLEEPING, DREAMING, AND DYING
An Exploration of Consciousness with the Dalai Lama
Edited by Francisco Varela

About Wisdom Publications

Wisdom Publications is the leading publisher of classic and contemporary Buddhist books and practical works on mindfulness. To learn more about us or to explore our other books, please visit our website at wisdomexperience.org or contact us at the address below.

Wisdom Publications
199 Elm Street
Somerville, MA 02144 USA

We are a 501(c)(3) organization, and donations in support of our mission are tax deductible.

Wisdom Publications is affiliated with the Foundation for the Preservation of the Mahayana Tradition (FPMT).